Thomas Erskine

The inner life as revealed in the correspondence of celebrated Christians

Thomas Erskine

The inner life as revealed in the correspondence of celebrated Christians

ISBN/EAN: 9783337262174

Printed in Europe, USA, Canada, Australia, Japan

Cover: Foto ©Lupo / pixelio.de

More available books at **www.hansebooks.com**

THE INNER LIFE.

THE HOME LIBRARY.

THE INNER LIFE

AS REVEALED IN THE CORRESPONDENCE OF CELEBRATED CHRISTIANS.

EDITED BY

REV. T. ERSKINE.

PUBLISHED UNDER THE DIRECTION OF THE TRACT COMMITTEE.

LONDON:
SOCIETY FOR PROMOTING CHRISTIAN KNOWLEDGE;
SOLD AT THE DEPOSITORIES:
77, GREAT QUEEN STREET, LINCOLN'S INN FIELDS;
4, ROYAL EXCHANGE; 48, PICCADILLY;
AND BY ALL BOOKSELLERS.

NEW YORK: POTT, YOUNG AND CO

1878.

LONDON:
PRINTED BY WILLIAM CLOWES AND SONS,
STAMFORD STREET AND CHARING CROSS.

PREFACE.

The Letters in this Volume were written exclusively by Members of the Church of England, but, as will be seen by the list, by men of very different schools of thought within the limits of that Church.

The Editor desires to express his thanks to the various Publishers and others, who have given him leave to make use of the works, the copyrights of which they hold. He has met with much kindness and sympathy, and with very few refusals.

LIST OF AUTHORS,

ARRANGED IN CHRONOLOGICAL ORDER, ACCORDING TO THE DATE OF THEIR BIRTH.

	PAGE
Rev. Henry Venn [1724–1797]	1
Rev. John Newton [1725–1807]	7
Rev. John William Fletcher [1729–1785]	37
William Cowper, the Poet [1731–1800]	57
Hannah More [1745–1833]	81
Rev. Charles Simeon [1758–1836]	85
Alexander Knox [1758–1831]	113
William Wilberforce [1759–1833]	123
Right Rev. D. Wilson, Bishop of Calcutta [1778–1857]	133
Rev. Henry Martyn [1781–1812]	143
Sir T. F. Buxton, Bart. [1786–1845]	177
Rev. John Keble [1792–1866]	189
Rev. T. Arnold, D.D. [1795–1842]	209
Maria Hare [1798–1870]	223
Sara Coleridge [1802–1851]	249

	PAGE
RIGHT REV. R. GRAY, BISHOP OF CAPETOWN [1809–1872]	263
REV. T. G. RAGLAND [1815–1858]	281
REV. F. W. ROBERTSON [1816–1853]	291
REV. R. A. SUCKLING [1818–1851]	303
REV. C. KINGSLEY [1819–1875]	319
CAPTAIN HEDLEY VICARS [1826–1855]	335
RIGHT REV. J. C. PATTESON, MISSIONARY BISHOP [1827–1871]	353

BOOKS FROM WHICH THE LETTERS ARE TAKEN.

"Life of Rev. Henry Venn."

Rev. J. Newton's "Cardiphonia."

Rev. J. Newton's "Letters to a Wife."

Rev. J. Newton's "Letters."

Rev. J. W. Fletcher's "Works."

"Life of Rev. J. W. Fletcher."   An American publication.

"Life of Rev. J. W. Fletcher."   By Wesley.

"Life of William Cowper."   By Southey.

"Life of William Cowper."   By Rev. T. S. Grimshawe.

"Life of Hannah More," and "Mendip Annals."

"Life of Rev. C. Simeon."   By Rev. Canon Carus.

Alexander Knox's "Remains."

"Life of William Wilberforce."   By his Sons.

"Life of Right Rev. D. Wilson."   By Rev. J. Bateman.

"Life of Rev. Henry Martyn."

"Life of Sir T. F. Buxton, Bart."   By his Son.

Rev. John Keble's "Letters of Spiritual Counsel."

"Life of Rev. T. Arnold."   By A. P. Stanley.

Maria Hare's "Memorials of a Quiet Life."

"Memoir of Sara Coleridge." By her Daughter.

"Life of Right Rev. Bishop Gray." By his Son.

"Life of Rev. T. G. Ragland." By Rev. T. T. Perowne.

"Memoir of Rev. F. W. Robertson."

"Life of Rev. R. A. Suckling."

Rev. C. Kingsley, "His Letters, and Memories of his Life." Edited by his Wife.

"Life of Captain Hedley Vicars." By Miss Marsh.

"Life of Right Rev. J. C. Patteson." By Miss Yonge.

HENRY VENN.

THE INNER LIFE.

I.

HENRY VENN was born in March, 1724, and ordained in 1747. In 1759 he was appointed Vicar of Huddersfield, from which he moved to Yelling, in 1771, in consequence of a threatened failure of health. He died in 1797.

TO A YOUNG FRIEND.

November, 1768.

Several things, of late, have put me, my dear sir, into apprehensions of your spiritual welfare; particularly your absenting yourself from the Lord's Table on Sunday. I feel for your temptations, and I pray for you. But turn not from the God of all grace, give not up the use of the means of grace, whatever may have been your falls, whatever are the accusations of your conscience, however strong and violent your corruptions. It is the cruel suggestion of Satan which tells you there is no help for you in your God, that so long as you have striven, and not yet got the mastery over your besetting sin, it is in vain to strive any longer; for in Christ Jesus there is plenteous redemption; and, though He often suffers us to be wounded, and terribly too, yet He will heal, He will deliver the praying soul, those that are bowed down with the weight and chain of their sin. If you, alas! fall into wilful transgression, do not make it worse by rejecting the only possible remedy. If you are overcome of presumptuous wickedness, run to Jesus with your wounds bleeding, your conscience accusing, and under all the aggravations of guilt which can possibly attend your fall. He has a heart to forgive *all* affronts put upon Him, all the most heinous provocations, and the most shocking injuries the devil can tempt poor sinners to commit. Will you, then, my dear young man—in whom I have taken so much pleasure, as one devoting yourself in the flower of youth to Jesus—will you forsake Him? When He is the person injured, and yet waits to be gracious, will you, the aggressor, be such a foe to yourself as not to go to Him for pardon? When He, whom your righteousness cannot profit, promises to love you freely and heal your backslidings, and be a covert to you from the wind of temptation, will you, who stand in absolute need of these mercies, keep away? . . . Tell Him it is impossible for you to resist the devil, and your own desperately wicked heart, in any strength of your own. . . . I have had myself many a sore and dreadful conflict before the time of my redemption came. . . . Put the case that, uneasy and galled with the sight and sense of your own provocations, you fly from Christ, you leave off receiving the Sacrament, reading God's Word, and prayer. Alas! I am ready to weep at the terrible consequences: sin and Satan must then necessarily prevail; conscience will become a sharp accuser, and haunt you as a ghost; you will expose the cause of Christ to shame and reproach amongst His enemies; you will discourage the young people who have begun to run well; you will contribute to keep in their revolt from God those who have, alas! turned back to folly; you will be ashamed of seeing your companions in the good ways of the Lord; you will fear death, and be in a manner forced to fly for refuge (how different a refuge from the loving Jesus!) to those of a scared conscience and profligate life, in order to drown convictions. . . . The Lord give you understanding to ponder these things; to read what I have offered in the same spirit of love which made me write it, and in prayer to God for a blessing upon this endeavour of your minister, who watches for your soul as one that must give account.

JOHN NEWTON.

II.

THE Rev. JOHN NEWTON was born in 1725, was ordained in 1764, Curate at Olney till 1779, Rector of St. Mary Woolnoth 1779, died 1807. Letters taken from "The Cardiphonia."

LETTER TO MR. B——.

1774.

I see the necessity of having, if possible, my principles at my fingers' ends, that I may apply them as occasions arise every hour. Certainly if my ability were equal to my inclination, I would remove your tumour with a word or a touch; I would exempt you instantly and constantly from every inconvenience and pain; but you are in the hands of One who could do all this and more, and who loves you infinitely better than I can do, and yet He is pleased to permit you to suffer. What is the plain inference? Certainly that, at the present juncture, He, to whom all the concatenations and consequences of events are present in our view, sees it better for you to have this tumour than to be without it; for I have no more idea of a tumour arising (or any other incidental trial befalling you) without a cause, without a need-be, without a designed advantage to result from it, than I have of a mountain or pyramid rising up of its own accord in the midst of Salisbury Plain. The promise is express, and literally true, that all things, universally and without exception, shall work together for good to them that love God. But they work *together*—the smallest as well as the greatest events have their place and use; like the several stones in the arch of a bridge, where no one would singly be useful, but every one in its place is necessary to the structure and support of the arch; or rather like the movement of a watch, where, though there is an evident subordination of parts, and some pieces have a greater comparative importance than others, yet the smallest pieces have their place and use, and are so far equally important, that the whole design of the machine would be obstructed for want of them. Some dispensations and turns of Providence may be compared to the main-spring or capital wheels, which have a more visible, sensible, and determining influence on the whole tenor of our lives; but the more ordinary occurrences of every day are at least pins and pivots, adjusted, tuned, and suited with equal accuracy by the hand of the same great Artist who planned and executes the whole; and we are sometimes surprised to see how much more depends and turns upon them than we are aware of. Then we admire His skill, and say He has done all things well. . . . Such thoughts as these, when I am enabled to realize them, in some measure reconcile me to what He allots to myself or my friends, and convince me of the propriety of that expostulation, which speaks the language of love as well as of authority, "Be still, and know that I am God."

I sympathize with you in your trial, and pray and trust that your Shepherd will be your Physician, will superintend and bless the use of means, will give you in His good time health and cure, and at all times reveal unto you abundance of peace. His promises and power are necessary for our preservation in the smoother scenes He has allotted for us, and they are likewise sufficient for the roughest. We are always equally in danger in ourselves, and always equally safe under the shadow of His wings.

To the Same.

October, 1774.

I think the greatness of trials is to be estimated rather by the impression they make upon our spirits, than by their outward appearance. The smallest will be too heavy for us if we are left to grapple with it in our own strength, or rather weakness; and if the Lord is pleased to put forth His power in us, He can make the heaviest light. A lively impression of His love, or of the glories within the vail, accompanied with a due sense of the miseries from which we are redeemed; these thoughts will enable us to be not only submissive but even joyful in tribulations. When faith is in exercise, though the flesh will have its feelings, the spirit will triumph over them. But it is needful we should know we have no sufficiency in ourselves, and in order to know it we must feel it, and therefore the Lord sometimes withdraws His sensible influence, and then the buzzing of a fly will be an over-match for our patience; at other times He will show what He can do in us and for us. . . . It is observable that the children of God seldom disappoint our expectations under great trials; if they show a wrongness of spirit it is usually in such little incidents that we are ready to wonder at them. For which, two reasons may be principally assigned. When great trials are in view, we run simply and immediately to our all-sufficient Friend, feel our dependence, and cry in good earnest for help; but if the occasion seem small, we are too apt secretly to lean to our own wisdom and strength, as if, in such slight matters, we could make shift without Him. Therefore in these we often fail. Again, the Lord deals with us as we sometimes see mothers with their children. When a child begins to walk he is often very self-important; he thinks he needs no help, and can hardly bear to be supported by the finger of another. Now in such a case, if there is no danger or harm from a fall, the mother will let him alone, to try how he can walk. . . . But were he upon the brink of a river or a precipice, from whence a fall might be fatal, the tender mother would not trust him to himself, no, not for a moment. I have not room to make the application, nor is it needful. It requires the same grace to bear with a right spirit a cross word as a cross injury, or the breaking of a china plate as the death of an only son.

LETTER TO THE REV. MR. P——.

January 11, 1777.

If, as you observe, the Song of Solomon describes the experience of His Church, it shows the dark as well as the bright side. No one part of it is the experience of every individual at any particular time. Some are in His banqueting house, others in their beds. Some sit under His banner supported by His arm, while others have a faint perception of Him at a distance, with many a hill and mountain between. In one thing, however, they all agree, that He is the leading object of their desires, and that they have made such a discovery of His person, work, and love, as makes Him precious to their hearts. Their judgment of Him is always the same, but their sensibility varies. The love they bear Him, though rooted and grounded in their hearts, is not always equally in exercise, nor indeed can it be so. We are like trees which, though alive, cannot put forth their leaves and fruit without the influence of the sun. They are alive in winter as well as in summer, but how different is their appearance in these different seasons! Were we always alike, could we always believe, love, rejoice, we should think the power inherent and our own; but it is more for the Lord's glory, and more suited to form us to a temper becoming the gospel, that we should be made deeply sensible of our own inability and dependence, than that we should be always in a lively frame.... A soul may be in as thriving a state when thirsting, seeking, and mourning after the Lord, as when actually rejoicing in Him; as much in earnest when fighting in the valley, as when singing on the mount; nay, dark seasons afford the surest and strongest manifestations of the power of faith. To hold fast the word of promise, to maintain a hatred of sin, to go on stedfastly in the path of duty, in defiance both of the frowns and smiles of the world, when we have but little comfort, is a much more certain evidence of grace than a thousand things which we may do or forbear when our spirits are warm and lively.

To Miss F——.

March, 1779.

Our experiences pretty much tally; they may be drawn out into sheets and quires, but the sum total may be described in a short sentence, "Our life is a warfare." For our encouragement the apostle calls it a *good* warfare. We are engaged in a good cause, fight under a good Captain, the victory is sure beforehand, and the prize is a crown, a crown of life. Such considerations might make even a coward bold. But then we must be content to fight; and considering the nature, number, situation, and subtlety of our enemies, we may expect sometimes to receive a wound; but there is a medicinal tree, the leaves of which are always at hand to heal us. We cannot be too attentive to the evil which is always working in us, or to the stratagems which are employed against us; yet our attention should not be wholly confined to these things. We are to look upwards likewise to Him who is our Head, our Life, our Strength. . . . One great cause of our frequent conflicts is, that we have a secret desire to be rich, and it is the Lord's design to make us poor. *We* want to gain an ability of doing something, and He suits His dispensations to convince us that we can do nothing. *We* want a stock in ourselves, and He would have us absolutely dependent upon Him. So far as we are content to be weak, that His power may be magnified in us, so far we shall make our enemies know that we are strong, though we ourselves shall never be directly sensible that we are so; only by comparing what we are with the opposition we stand against, we may come to a comfortable conclusion that the Lord worketh mightily in us.

To Mr. A. B——.

1758.

I suppose you will receive many congratulations on your recovery from your late dangerous illness, most of them, perhaps, more sprightly and better turned, but none, I persuade myself, more sincere and affectionate, than mine. I beg you would prepare yourself by this good opinion of me before you read further; and let the reality of my regard excuse what you may dislike in my manner of expressing it.

When a person has returned from a doubtful, distant voyage, we are naturally led to inquire into the incidents he has met with, and the discoveries he has made. Indulge me in a curiosity of this kind, especially as my affection gives me an interest and concern in the event. You have been, my friend, upon the brink, the very edge of an eternal state; but God has restored you back to the world again. Did you meet with, or have you brought back, anything *new?* Did nothing occur to stop or turn your usual train of thought? Were your apprehensions of invisible things exactly the same in the height of your disorder, when you were cut off from the world and all its engagements, as when you were in perfect health, and in the highest enjoyment of your inclinations? If you answer me, "Yes, all things are just the same as formerly, the difference between sickness and health alone excepted," I am at a loss how to reply. I can only sigh and wonder: *sigh*, that it should be thus with any, that it should be thus with you whom I dearly love; and *wonder*, since this unhappy case, strange as it seems in one view, is yet so frequent, why it was not always thus with myself—for long and often it was just so. Many a time, when sickness had brought me, as we say, to death's door, I was as easy and as insensible as the sailor, who in the height of a storm should presume to sleep upon the top of the mast, quite regardless that the next tossing wave might plunge him into the raging ocean, beyond all possibility of relief. But at length a day came, which, though the most terrible day I ever saw, I can now look back upon with thankfulness and pleasure; I say the time came when, in such a helpless extremity, and under the expectation of immediate death, it pleased God to command the veil from my eyes, and I saw things in some measure as they really were. Imagine with yourself a person trembling upon the point of a dreadful precipice, a powerful and inexorable enemy ready to push him down, and an assemblage of all that is horrible waiting at the bottom for his fall; even this will give you but a faint representation of the state of my mind at that time. Believe me, it was not a whim or a dream, which changed my sentiments and my conduct, but a powerful conviction, which will not admit of the least doubt—an evidence which, like that I have of my own existence, I cannot call in question without contradicting my senses. And though my case was in some respects uncommon, yet something like it is known by one and another every day. . . . By these instances I know that nothing is too hard for the Almighty. The same power which humbled me can doubtless bring down the most haughty infidel upon earth, as I likewise know that, to show forth His power, He is often pleased to make use of weak instruments. I am encouraged, notwithstanding the apparent difficulty of succeeding, to warn those over whom friendship or affection gives me influence, of the evil and danger of a course of life formed upon the prevailing maxims of the world. So far as I neglect this I am unfaithful in my professions both to God and man. . . . I used a wrong word when I spoke of your *recovery*. My dear friend, look upon it only as a *reprieve*, for you carry the sentence of death about with you still; and unless you should be cut off (which God of His mercy forbid!) by a sudden stroke, you will as surely lie upon a death-bed as you have now been raised from a bed of sickness. And remember, likewise (how can I bear to write?) that, should you neglect my admonitions, they will, notwithstanding, have an effect upon you, though not such an effect as I could wish; they will render you more inexcusable. I have delivered my own soul by faithfully warning you; but if you will not examine the matter with that seriousness it calls for; if you will not look up to God, the Former of your body and the preserver of your spirit, for direction and assistance how to please Him; if you will have your reading and conversation only on one side of the question; if you determine to let afflictions and dangers, mercies and deliverances, all pass without reflection and improvement; if you will spend your life as though you thought you were sent into the world only to eat, sleep, and play, and after a course of years be extinguished like the snuff of a candle;—why then you must abide the consequences. But assuredly, sooner or later, God will meet you. My hearty daily prayer is that it may be in a way of mercy, and that you may be added to the number of the trophies of His invincible grace.

LETTER TO THE REV. MR. B——.

April 16, 1772.

I hope the Lord has contracted my desires and aims almost to the one point of study, the knowledge of His truth. All other acquisitions are transient, and comparatively vain. And yet, alas! I am a slow scholar, nor can I see in what respect I get forward, unless that every day I am more confirmed in the conviction of my own emptiness and inability to all spiritual good. And as, notwithstanding this, I am still enabled to stand my ground, I would hope, since no effect can be without some adequate cause, that I have made some advance, though in a manner imperceptible to myself, towards a more simple dependence upon Jesus as my all in all. It is given me to thirst and to taste, if it is not given me to drink abundantly; and I would be thankful for the desire. I see and approve the wisdom, grace, suitableness, and sufficiency of the gospel salvation; and since it is for sinners, and I am a sinner, and the promises are open, I do not hesitate to call it mine. I am a weary laden soul, Jesus has invited me to come, and has enabled me to put my trust in Him. I seldom have an uneasy doubt, at least not of any continuance, respecting my pardon, acceptance, and interest in all the blessings of the New Testament. And amidst a thousand infirmities and evils under which I groan, I have the testimony of my conscience, when under the trial of His Word, that my desire is sincerely towards Him, that I choose no other portion, and that I allowedly serve no other Master. When I told our friend —— lately to this purpose, he wondered, and asked, "How is it possible that, if you can see these things, you should not be always rejoicing?" Undoubtedly I derive from the gospel a peace at bottom which is worth more than a thousand worlds; but so it is, I can only speak for myself, though I rest and live upon the truths of the gospel, they seldom impress me with a warm and lively joy. In public, indeed, I sometimes seem in earnest and much affected, but even then it appears to me rather as a part of the gift intrusted to me for the edification of others, than as a sensation which is properly my own. For when I am in private I am usually dull and stupid to a strange degree, or the prey to a wild and ungoverned imagination, so that I may truly say when I would do good, evil, horrid evil, is present with me. Ah! how different is this from sensible comfort! And if I were to compare myself to others, to make their experience my standard, and was not helped to retreat to the sure Word of God as my refuge, how hard should I find it to maintain a hope that I had either part or lot in the matter! What I call my good times are, when I can find my attention in some little measure fixed to what I am about, which, indeed, is not always nor frequently my case in prayer, and still seldomer in reading the Scriptures. My judgment embraces these as blessed privileges, and Satan has not prevailed to drive me from them; but in the performance

I too often find them tasks, feel a reluctance when the seasons return, and am glad when they are finished. Oh what a mystery is the heart of man! What a warfare is the life of faith!—at least in the path the Lord is pleased to lead me. What reason have I to lie in the dust as the chief of sinners! and what cause for thankfulness that salvation is wholly of grace! Notwithstanding all my complaints, it is still true that Jesus died and rose again, that He ever liveth to make intercession, and is able to save to the uttermost. But on the other hand, to think of that joy of heart in which some of His people live, and to compare it with that apparent deadness and want of spirituality which I feel, this makes me mourn. However, I think there is a Scriptural distinction between faith and feeling, grace and comfort; they are not inseparable, and perhaps, when together, the degree of the one is not often the just measure of the other. But though I pray that I may be ever longing and panting for the light of His countenance, yet I would be so far satisfied as to believe the Lord has wise and merciful reasons for keeping me so short of the comforts which He has taught me to desire and value more than the light of the sun.

LETTER TO MRS. ——.

July, 1764.

The complaints you make are inseparable from a spiritual acquaintance with our own hearts. I would not wish you to be less affected with a sense of in-dwelling sin. It becomes us to be humbled to the dust; yet our grief, though it cannot be too great, may be under a wrong direction; and if it leads us to impatience or distrust, it certainly is so. Sin is the sickness of the soul, in itself mortal and incurable as to any power in heaven or earth but that of the Lord Jesus only. But He is the great, the infallible Physician. Have we the privilege to know His name? Have we been enabled to put ourselves under His hand? We have, then, no more to do but to attend to His prescriptions, to be satisfied with His methods, and to wait His time. It is lawful to wish we were well; it is natural to groan being burdened; but still He must and will take His own course with us, and however dissatisfied with ourselves, we ought still to be thankful that He has begun His work in us, and to believe that He will also make an end. ... Again, some of the first prayers which the Spirit of God teaches us to put up are for a clearer sense of the sinfulness of sin, and our vileness on account of it. Now if the Lord is pleased to answer your prayers in this respect, though it will afford you cause enough for humiliation, yet it should be received likewise with thankfulness as a token for good. Your heart is not worse than it was formerly, only your spiritual knowledge is increased, and this is no small part of the growth in grace which you are thirsting after, to be truly humbled, and emptied, and made little in your own eyes. Further, the examples of the saints recorded in Scripture prove (and, indeed, of the saints in general) that the greater measure any person has of the grace of God, in truth, the more lively and conscientious they have been, and the more they have been favoured with assurances of the Divine favour—so much the more deep and sensible their perception of in-dwelling sin and infirmity has always been; so it was with Job, Isaiah, Daniel, and Paul. It is likewise common to overcharge ourselves. Indeed, we cannot think worse of ourselves than we really are; yet some things which abate the comfort and alacrity of our Christian profession are rather impediments than properly sinful, and will not be imputed to us by Him who knows our frame, and remembers that we are but dust. Thus to have an infirm memory, to be subject to disordered, irregular, or low spirits, are faults of the constitution, in which the *will* has no share; though they are all burdensome and oppressive, and sometimes needlessly so, by our charging ourselves with guilt on their account. The same may be observed of the unspeakable and fierce suggestions of Satan, with which some persons are pestered, but which shall be laid to him from whom they proceed, and not to them who are troubled and terrified because they are forced to feel them. Lastly, it is by the experience of these evils within ourselves, and by feeling our utter insufficiency, either to perform duty or to withstand our enemies, that the Lord takes occasion to show us the suitableness, the sufficiency, the freeness, the unchangeableness, of His power and grace. This is the inference St. Paul draws from his complaints (Rom. vii. 25), and he learnt it upon a trying occasion from the Lord's own mouth (2 Cor. xii. 8, 9).

Let us then, dear madam, be thankful and cheerful, and, while we take shame to ourselves, let us glorify God by giving Jesus the honour due to His name. Though we are poor, He is rich; though we are weak, He is strong; though we have nothing, He possesses all things. He suffered for us; He calls us to be conformed to His sufferings. He conquered in His own person, and He will make each of His members more than conquerors in due season. It is good to have one eye upon ourselves, but the other should be ever fixed on Him who stands in the relation of Saviour, Husband, Head, and Shepherd. In Him we have righteousness, peace, and power; He can control all that we fear; so that if our path should be through the fire or through the water, neither the flood shall drown us nor the flame kindle upon us; and ere long He will cut short our conflicts and say, "Come up hither." "Then shall our grateful songs abound, and every tear be wiped away." Having such promises and assurances, let us lift up our banner in His name, and pass on through every discouragement.

Letters to his Wife.

London, July 4, 1760.

You did not bid me write, because I suppose you hardly thought I could refrain, for so many tedious days, from giving my mind a little vent. How often have I told you, that whatever pleasure or amusement I may find in the company of friends, yet there is a peculiar something, that shares in and gives an inexpressible cast to every motion of my mind, when you are absent? A man deprived of his right hand may go about his business with the same spirit and alacrity as in time past; yet everything he undertakes will necessarily remind and convince him of his loss. This, or something like it, I may have hinted a thousand times; but as I write and speak from my heart, the thought occurs as readily to me as at the first, and I cannot easily avoid repeating it. I am afraid of idolatry; I am afraid we have been, and still are, too guilty of the charge; and the Lord, to whom alone we belong, and to whom all our services and affections are primarily due, might justly, very justly, blast our boasted paradise. Yet we owe it to Him that our souls are susceptive of tender and generous feelings. He formed us for each other, and His good providence brought us together. It is no wonder, if so many years, so many endearments, so many obligations, have produced an uncommon effect, and that by long habit; it has become almost impossible for me to draw a breath in which you are not concerned. If this mutual affection leads us to the fountain from whence our blessings flow, and if we can regard each other, and everything about us, with a reference to that eternity to which we are hasting, then are we happy indeed. Then not even Death (the dread of mortals, especially of those who live in the possession of their wishes), can greatly harm us. Death itself can only part us for a little space, as the pier of a bridge divides the stream for a few moments, but cannot make a real separation. The friendly waters soon mix again, and, with one force and consent, press forward to the ocean.

Were it not for the support of believing that there is a brighter and a longer day beyond the grave, I should sink down in despair, and starve, if I may use a vulgar saying, in the midst of plenty. For though I have known too much not to smile at the cold disciples (if there are any such) of Platonic love; yet methinks a regard like ours is designed to flourish in a better world than this, and can never appear displayed to its full extent and advantage, until transplanted into those regions of light and joy, where all that is imperfect and transient shall be no more known. Here, then, is the true plan of happiness for us; to consider that God who made us, made us immortals, and appointed us to spend so many years in the most interesting connection, not only to sweeten the cares of life, and to render our path through this wilderness more easy, but chiefly that we might be helpful in animating each other in our progress to that kingdom and crown which is incorruptible and undefiled—a kingdom to which we are called by Him who died once to give us right, and now lives for ever to give us entrance.

Olney, September 12.

I pray God to bless to you the ordinances and conversation you are favoured with in London, that you may go into Kent filled with the spirit of truth and love. When you are there I hope you will make good use of the Bible, and throne of grace, to preserve you from being infected by the spirit of the world. Ah, what a poor vain thing is the world! We have both found it so at times (though we once loved it), and shall find it so again. But may the Lord keep us alive to a sense of its vanity, before more evil days return to extort the confession from our feelings! Sickness and pain and a near prospect of death force upon the mind a conviction of the littleness and vanity of a worldly life. But there is a more pleasing way of learning this lesson, if we pay due attention to the Word of God, and pray for the light of His countenance. If He is pleased to make His face to shine upon us, all that the world can offer to bribe us will appear insignificant and trivial as the sports of children.

He who has given us this desire, will, I trust, answer it, and unite our souls to Himself for ever. Happy state! To have peace with God, by Jesus Christ; liberty of access to a throne of grace; an interest in all the promises; a sure guide by the way; and a sure inheritance at our journey's end! These things were once hidden from us. We were so blinded by the god of this world, that we could look no further than the present life. But, even then, the Lord looked upon us with an eye of mercy. He led us on gradually, by a way which we knew not, to bring us into the paths of peace. How wonderful has our history been, not mine only, but also yours! How often has He made Himself known as your Deliverer and Physician, in raising you up from the gates of the grave! May we always remember His goodness in your last affliction! How did He sweeten the bitter cup; strengthen you with strength in your soul; enable you to pray for yourself; engage the hearts of many in prayer for you, and then speedily answer our prayers! Let us, then, excite each other to praise Him! I hope this little interval of absence will be useful, to make me more sensible of His goodness in still sparing you to me. I make but a poor shift without you now from day to day; but I am comforted by the hope of seeing you again shortly. Had you been removed by your late fever, I should not have had this relief. May we then live to Him, and may every day be a preparation for the parting hour! Dark as this hour seems in the prospect, if we are established in the faith and hope of our Lord, we shall find it supportable; and the separation will be short. We shall soon meet again; happy meeting! to part no more; to be for ever with the Lord; to join in an eternal song to Him who loved us, and washed us from our sins in His own blood. Then all tears shall be wiped from our eyes, and we shall weep no more for ever.

Olney, November 21.

W. and R. B—— sent me word that their little girl was dying, and I have since heard she is dead. I expect to find them in much trouble. Thus, at one time or another, every family and every person finds vanity entwined with their choicest comforts. It is best for us that it is so; for, poor and vain as this life is, we are sufficiently attached to it. How strong, then, would our attachment be, if we met with no rubs or thorns by the way! Is not the history of every day a comment upon those words, "This is not your rest"? I think you and I must acknowledge that the Lord has given us, from the beginning of our union, a favoured lot. I think we have experienced as much of the good, and as few of the evils of life, as any persons whom we know. And yet, if we could fairly estimate all the pains, anxieties, and crosses we have met with, from first to last, it would make a considerable abatement in what, when taken in a more general view, may well be deemed a happy state. And how soon has the best of it passed away! Nothing now remains of many endeared hours, but the remembrance. Though we have had the best that such a life can afford, it would be a poor happiness indeed were this our all. But blessed be God, who has given us better hope than we had when we set out; for I think we then proposed no higher satisfaction than we could find in each other. It was well for us both that I was constrained to leave you for three long voyages; for though those frequent separations were very irksome at the time, they were sanctified to make us look further. Oh! He has led us wisely and graciously! He has done all things well. We have nothing now to ask, but for a deeper and more thankful sense of His goodness.

LETTERS TO FRIENDS.

August 13, 1773.

MY DEAR SIR,

We are always glad to hear from you, because your paper is perfumed with the name of Jesus. You speak well of Him, and you have reason, for He has been a good Friend to you. I likewise am enabled to say something of Him, and I trust the chief reason why I would wish my life to be prolonged is, that I may employ more of my breath in His praise. But, alas! while I endeavour to persuade others that He is the chief among ten thousand, and altogether lovely, I seem to be but half persuaded of it myself; I feel my heart so cold and unbelieving. But I hope I can say this is not I, but sin that dwelleth in me. Did you ever see my picture? I have it drawn by a masterly hand; and though another person, and one whom I am far from resembling, sat for it, it is as like me as one new guinea is like another. The original was drawn at Corinth, and sent to some persons of distinction at Rome. Many copies have been taken, and though, perhaps, it is not to be seen in any of the London print shops, it has a place in most public and private libraries, and I would hope in most families. I had seen it a great many times before I could discover one of my own features in it; but then my eyes were very bad. What is remarkable, it was drawn long before I was born, but having been favoured with some excellent eye-salve, I quickly knew it to be my own. I am drawn in an attitude which would be strange and singular, if it were not so common with me, looking two different and opposite ways at once, so that you would be puzzled to tell whether my eyes are fixed upon heaven or upon the earth; I am aiming at things inconsistent with each other at the same instant, so that I can accomplish neither. According to the different light in which you view the picture, I appear to rejoice and to mourn, to choose and to refuse, to be a conqueror or a captive—in a word, I am a double person, a riddle; it is no wonder if you know not what to make of me, for I cannot tell what to make of myself. I would and I would not; I do and I do not; I can and I cannot. I find the hardest things easy, and the easiest things impossible; but while I am in this perplexity you will observe in the same piece a hand stretched forth for my relief, and may see a label proceeding out of my mouth, "I thank God through Jesus Christ my Lord." The more I study this picture the more I discover some new and striking resemblance, which convinces me that the painter knew me better than I know myself.

November 27, 1767.

My dear Friend,

I congratulate you and Mrs. —— on your settlement at B——, in your new house, where I hope the Lord will dwell with and bless you both, and make you blessings to many.

Visits, etc., of ceremony are burdensome; yet

something is due to civility; and although we cannot have equal comfort in all our acquaintance, it is best to be on peaceful and neighbourly terms. You need not have much of it, but as far as it cannot be prudently avoided, bear it as your cross. I would not wish to have you attempt to force spiritual things too much upon those who do not like them; or to expect them from those who have not experienced them. But, like a physician among sick people, watch opportunities of doing them good if possible.

You know not what the Lord has to do; some whom you now can hardly bear, may prove your comforts hereafter; and if in the mean time they are disposed to be friendly, and show you good offices, they have a right to a return in the same way.

I approve and rejoice in your faithfulness; but in some things, perhaps, you would do as well to keep your mind more to yourself; I mean in your free and unreserved speaking of ministers, etc. Our Lord's direction to His disciples, in something of a similar case, was, Let them alone. So far as it is needful to withstand them, do so in the Lord's strength; but in mixed conversation it is a good rule to say nothing, without a just call, to the disadvantage of others.

September 4, 1778.

My dear Friend,

Welcome from K——. I hope you were the instrument of much good abroad, and brought home much comfort and peace in your own heart.

How many are the seen and the unseen mercies we are favoured with in a long journey! And what mercy to find Mrs. S—— and your family well on your return, as I hope you did! The same good Providence which has preserved you and yours, has taken care of me and mine. But Mrs. —— has been sometimes ill; no oftener and no more than we have been able to bear, or than the Lord saw was for our advantage. After so many years' experience of His goodness, we surely have reason to be convinced that He does all things well. At present, she is tolerably well.

We are His sheep; He is our Shepherd. If a sheep had reason, and were sensible of its own state, how weak to withstand the wolf, how prone in itself to wander, how utterly unable to provide for its own subsistence—it would have no comfort, unless it knew that it was under the care of a shepherd; and in proportion to the opinion it formed of the shepherd's watchfulness and sufficiency, such would be its confidence and peace. But if you could suppose the sheep had depravity likewise, then it would act as we often do—its reason would degenerate into vain reasoning; it would distrust the shepherd, and find fault with his management; it would burden itself with contrivances and cares; tremble under the thoughts of a hard winter, and never be easy unless it was surrounded with hay-stacks; it would study from morning till night where to hide itself out of the wolf's way. Poor, wise, silly sheep! If thou hadst not a shepherd, all thy schemes would be fruitless; when thou hast broken thy heart with care, thou art still as unable to preserve thyself as thou wast before; and if thou hast a good Shepherd, they are all needless. Is it not sufficient that He careth for thee?

Thus I would preach to such a sheep as I have supposed; and thus I preach to my own heart. But though I know I cannot, by any study of mine, add a cubit or an inch to my stature, I am prone to puzzle myself about twenty things, which are equally out of my power, and equally unnecessary if the Lord be my Shepherd.

December 3, 1780.

My dear Sir,

The Lord is risen indeed! This is His day, when we are called to meet in His house, and (we in this branch of His family) to rejoice at His Table. I meant to write yesterday, but could not. I trust it is not unsuitable to the design and privilege of this day, to give you a morning salutation in His name, and to say, "Come, magnify the Lord with me, and let us exalt His name together." If I am not mistaken I have met you this morning already. Were you not at Gethsemane? Have you not been to Golgotha? Did I not see you at the tomb? This is our usual circuit, yours and mine, on these mornings; indeed every morning; for what other places are worth visiting? what other objects are worth seeing? Oh, this wonderful love! this blood of sovereign efficacy! the infallible antidote which kills sin, cures the sinner, gives sight to the blind, and life to the dead! How often have I known it turn sorrow into joy!

O thou Saviour and Sun of the soul, shine forth this morning, and cheer and gladden all our hearts! Shine upon me and mine, upon all whom I love, and on all who love Thee! Shine powerfully on my dear friends at ——, and let us know that, though we are absent from each other, Thou art equally near to us all.

I must to breakfast, then dress, and away to court. Oh for a sight of the King! and, oh to hear Him speak! for His voice is music, and His person is beauty. When He says, Remember Me, and the heart hears, what a train of incidents is at once revived!—from the manger to the cross; what He said, what He did, how He lived, how He loved, how He died! all is marvellous, affecting, humbling, transporting. I think I know what I would be, and what I would do, too, if I could. How near would I get, how low would I fall, how would I weep and sing in a breath! and with what solemn earnestness would I recommend Him to my fellow-sinners! But alas! when I would do good, evil is present with me. Pray for me, and help me likewise to praise the Lord, for His mercies are new every morning and every moment.

I am your affectionate

JOHN WILLIAM FLETCHER.

III.

JOHN WILLIAM FLETCHER (F. G. DE LA FLECHERE) was born in Switzerland, in 1729. He tried to enter first the Portuguese, afterwards the Dutch, army. He then came to England, and became tutor in the family of Mr. HILL, M.P. for Shrewsbury. In 1757 he was ordained, but without any curacy. In 1758 he became Vicar of Madeley, in Shropshire, where he died in 1785.

TO THE REV. CHARLES WESLEY.

October 24, 1759.

MY DEAR SIR,

For some days past the hope of hearing from you has been balanced by the fear that you were not in a condition to write. This last idea prevails so much, that I take my pen to entreat you to deliver me from the inquietude which I suffer from your silence. If the gout prevents you from writing, employ the hand of a friend. If you are in the third heaven of contemplation and love, let brotherly love, for a moment, bring you down; if you wander in the desert of temptation, let sympathy unite you to a miserable man, who feels himself undone. Since my last, I have taken some steps towards the knowledge of myself. If you inquire what I have learned, I answer that I am naked of everything but pride and unbelief. Yesterday I was seized with the desire of making rhymes, and I versified my thoughts on the present state of my soul in a hymn, the first part of which I now send you. If the poetry does not deserve reading, the language will call to mind your French. May the care you take of your health have the success I wish; and while I wait the event, may He who enabled St. Paul to say, "When I am weak, then am I strong," sustain you in all your infirmities, and fill your inward man with His mighty power! At the moment I was going to seal mine, I received your dear letter. You will see by the hymn, in which I have attempted to paint my heart, that I have at present far other things to do than to think of going on to perfection, even laying the foundation of the spiritual house; much less, then, can I help forward those who seek it.

I am, etc.,
J. Fletcher.

To Miss Hatton.

Madeley, December, 1764.

Madam,

I am sensible how much I want advice in a thousand particulars, and how incapable I am safely to direct any one; I shall, nevertheless, venture to throw upon this sheet the following observations, as they came to my mind on the reading your letter. You cannot expect, on the gospel plan, to attain to such a carriage as will please all you converse with.

The Son of God, the original of all human perfection, was blamed sometimes for His silence, and sometimes for His speaking; and shall the handmaid be above her Master?

There is no sin in wearing such things as you have by you, if they are not out of character; I mean if they are necessary for your station, and characterize your rank. There is no sin in allowing yourself a little more latitude in speech, provided you listen to Christ, by inward attention to His teaching, and the end of what you say may be to introduce what is useful and edifying; for God judgeth of words according to the intention of the speaker. I may speak idly even in the pulpit; and I may speak to edification in the market, if what I say is either necessary or proper to introduce, or drive the nail of a profitable truth. Some parables of our Lord would have been deemed idle talk had it not been for the end He pursued, and, upon the whole, accomplished by them. No particular rule can be given here; a thousand circumstances of persons' tempers, places, times, states, etc., will necessarily vary a Christian's plan.

There is no sin in looking cheerful. No; it is our duty to be cheerful. Rejoice evermore; and if it is our duty to be always filled with joy, it is our duty to appear what we really are. I hope, however, your friends know how to distinguish between cheerfulness and levity.

If you want to recommend religion to those you converse with, and, in many instances, to pluck up offence by the root, let your heart lie where Mary's body did—keep close to Jesus; be attentive to His still, small voice, and He will fill you with humble love; and such love will teach you, without any rule, as by the instinct of your new nature, "To become all things to all men."

You ask what the apostle meant by that expression. It is certain he did not mean to overset his own precept, "Be not conformed to the world." I apprehend that in every case wherein we might promote the spiritual or temporal good of any one, by doing or suffering things of an indifferent nature, or even painful and disagreeable to us, we ought to be ready to become all things to all; provided the good we propose is superior to the inconveniences to which we submit. Here also we stand in need of humble love and meek wisdom, that we may so weigh circumstances, as to form a right judgment in all things.

I am glad the Lord strips you; I wish self may never clothe you again. Beware of stiff singularity in things barely indifferent—it is self in disguise; and it is so much the more dangerous, as it comes recommended by a serious, self-denying, religious appearance.

I hope the shortcomings of some about you will not prevent your eyeing the prize of a glorious conformity to our blessed Head. It is to be feared, that not a few of those who talk of having attained it, have mistaken the way; they are still something, and I apprehend an important step towards that conformity, is to become nothing! Or, rather, with St. Paul, to become in our own eyes the "chief of sinners," and the "least of saints."

To the Same.

Madeley, June 2, 1765.

Madam,

I thank you for the letter of your correspondent. What he says about luminous joys may sometimes be the case in some of God's dear children; but I apprehend that God's design in withholding from them those gracious influences, which work upon and melt the sensitive, affectionate part of the soul, is to put us more upon using the nobler powers, the understanding and the will. These are always more in the reach of a child of God, while the other greatly depends upon the texture of the animal frame; and if they are not stirred in a natural way, the Spirit of God can alone, without any concurrence, in general excite them. Do you believe love—take up your cross, and run after Jesus!

You must let friends and foes talk about your dress, while you mind only Jesus, His Word, and your own conscience. You talk of hearing me soon. I dare never invite any one to hear me, though I am glad to see my friends; but now I can invite you with pleasure to come and hear a preacher, who, under God, will make you amends for the trouble of a journey to Madeley.

His name is M——; he may possibly stay a Sunday or two more with me; but Jesus has promised to be always with His followers. To His merciful hands I commend you and your unworthy friend,

J. Fletcher.

To the Same.

Madeley, May 27, 1766.

My dear Friend,

I am glad to hear that the God of all mercies and grace has raised you from the bed of sickness, where His love had confined you. It is good to see His works in the deep, and then to come and sing His praises in the land of the living. A touch of pain or sickness I find always profitable to me, as it rivets on my soul the thoughts of my nothingness, helplessness, and mortality, and shows me in a clearer light the vanity of all the transitory scenes of life. May your afflictions have the same effect on you, as long as you live! May you be more stedfast than I am, to retain the deep impressions which God's gracious rod may have left upon your soul! And may you learn to lay yourself out more for the Lord, and to do whatsoever your hand findeth to do, with all your might, knowing that there is no wisdom nor device in the grave, whither we are going! If a sparrow falleth not to the ground, nor a hair from our heads, without our Heavenly Father's leave, it is certain that the higher circumstances of our life are planned by the wise and gracious Governor of all things. This kind of faith in Providence I find of indispensible necessity, to go calmly through life, and, I think too, through death also.

To Miss Ireland.

Madeley, July, 1766.

The poor account your father has brought us of your health, and his apprehensions of not seeing you any more before that solemn day, when all people, nations, and tongues shall stand together at the bar of God, make me venture (together with my love to you) to send you a few lines; and my earnest prayer to God is, that they may be blessed to your soul.

First, then, my dear friend, let me beseech you not to flatter yourself with the hopes of living long here on earth. These hopes fill us with worldly thoughts, and make us backward to prepare for our change. I would not for the world entertain such thoughts about myself. I have now in my parish a young man, who has been these two years under the surgeon's hand. Since they have given him up, which is about two months ago, he has fled to the Lord, and found in Him that saving health, which surpasses a thousand times that which the surgeons flattered him with; and he now longs to depart and be with Christ, which is far better. To see the bridge of life cut off behind us, and to have done with all the thoughts of repairing it to go back into the world, has a natural tendency to make us venture forward to the foot of the cross.

Secondly. Consider, my dear, how good the Lord is to call you to be transplanted into a better world before you have taken deeper root in this sinful world. And if it is too hard for nature to die now, how much harder do you think it would be if you lived to be the mother of a family, and to cleave to earth by the ties of many new relations, schemes of gain, or prospects of happiness!

Thirdly. Reflect by your illness, the Lord, the Lord who forecasts for us, intimates long life would not be for His glory nor your happiness. I believe He takes many young people from the evil to come, and out of the way of those temptations or misfortunes which would have made them miserable in time and in eternity.

Fourthly. Your earthly father loves you much; witness the hundreds of miles he has gone for the bare prospect of your health; but, my dear, your Heavenly Father loves you a thousand times better, and He is all wisdom as well as all goodness. Allow, then, such a loving, gracious Father, to choose for you; and if He chooses death, acquiesce and say, as you can, "Good is the will of the Lord; His choice must be best!"

Fifthly. Weigh the sinfulness of sin, both original and actual, and firmly believe the wages of sin is death. This will make you patiently accept the punishment, especially if you consider that Jesus Christ, by dying for us has taken away the sting of death, and turned the grave into a passage to a blessed eternity.

Sixthly. Beware of impatience, repining, and peevishness, which are the sins of sick people. Be gentle, easy to be pleased, and resigned as the bleeding Lamb of God. Wrong tempers indulged, grieve, if they do not quench, the Spirit.

Seventhly. Do not repine at being in a strange country, far from your friends; and, if your going to France does not answer the end proposed to your body, it will answer a spiritual end to our soul. God suffers the broken reeds of your acquaintance to be out of your reach, that you may not catch at them, and that you may, at once, cast your lonesome soul on the bosom of Him who fills heaven and earth.

Eighthly. In praying, reading, hearing any person read, and meditating, do not consult feeble, fainting, weary flesh and blood. For, at this rate, death may find you idle and supine, instead of striving to enter in at the strait gate; and when your spirits and vigour fail, remember that the Lord is the strength of your life, and your portion for ever. "O death, where is thy sting?" "Thanks be to God, who giveth us the victory through Jesus Christ our Lord!"

Many pray hard for you, that you may acquit yourself, living or dying, in ease or in pain, as a wise virgin, and as a good soldier of Jesus Christ; but, above all, Jesus the Captain of your salvation, and the High Priest of your profession, intercedes mightily for you. Look to Him and be saved, even from the ends of France. To His pity, love, and power I recommend you. May He bless you, my dear friend, and lift up the light of His countenance upon you, and give you peace, and courage, repentance, faith, hope, and patient love, both now and evermore.

I am your affectionate, sincere friend, and servant in Jesus,

J. FLETCHER.

To Miss Hatton.

Madeley, July 30, 1766.

My dear Friend,

So you are likely to be at rest first! Well, the Lord's will be done; I should be glad to have you stay to help us to the kingdom of God; but if God wants to take you there, and house you before a storm, I shall only cry, "One of the chariots of Israel and the horsemen thereof!" and try to make the best of my way after you.

A calm receiving of the gospel tidings, upon a conviction of your lost estate, with suitable tempers, is a sign that you are in a safe state; but I want you to be altogether in a comfortable one. Your business, I apprehend, is not to turn the dunghill of nature, but to suck the gospel milk. Dwell much, if not altogether, upon free justification "through the redemption that is in Christ Jesus." View the sufficiency, fulness, suitableness, freeness of His atonement and righteousness; and hide yourself without delay under both. Look at death only as a door to let you out of manifold infirmities and pains, into the arms of Jesus, your Heavenly Bridegroom. Stir up faith, hope, and love; that is trimming your lamp. Since last Monday, I find the burden of your soul upon mine in a very particular manner, and I hope that I shall not cease to pray for you, that you may go not only calmly, but joyfully, the way of all flesh. I have got some praying souls to share with me in that profitable work, and I hope you will meet our spirits at the throne of grace, as we do yours. Let me have the comfort of thinking that you are with your Physician, Husband, and all; who will order all things for the best. Pray hard, believe harder, and love hardest. Let the cry of your soul be, "None but Jesus living; none but Jesus dying." Let Christ be your life, and then your death, whether it comes sooner or later, will be your gain.

Mr. Glayebrook waits for these lines, and I conclude by again entreating you to believe—"Only believe," said Jesus to the ruler; and faith will work by love, and love by a desire to depart and be with Christ. God the Father, Son, and Holy Ghost, bless, uphold, and comfort you! Farewell, and forget not to pray for your helpless friend,

J. Fletcher.

To Miss Perronet.

Newington, April 21, 1777.

My dear Friend,

A thousand thanks to you for your kind, comfortable lines. This prospect of going to see Jesus and His glorified members, and among them your dear departed brother, my now ever-living friend—this sweet prospect is enough to make me quietly and joyfully submit to leave all my Shoreham friends and all the excellent of the earth. But why do I talk of going to leave any of Christ's members, by going to be more intimately united to the Head?

> "We all are one, who Him receive,
> And each with each agree;
> In Him the One, the Truth, we live,
> Blest point of unity!"

—A point this, which fills heaven and earth, which runs through time and eternity. What an immense point! In it sickness is lost in health, and death in life. There let us ever meet. There to live is Christ, and to die is gain. Thank dear Mrs. Bissaker for all her love to my dear departed friend; and may our kindred spirits drink deeper into God, till they are filled with all the fulness which our enlarged souls can admit. Nor let your niece, to whom I send my thanks, keep aloof. Let us all tend to our original centre; and experience that life and death are ours, because the Prince of Life has overcome sin, death, and the grave for you, and for your obliged, unworthy brother,

J. Fletcher.

To Mr. William Wase.
Nyon, Feb. 11, 1779.

My dear Friend,

I have just received yours of the 24th of January, and rejoice to hear of the welfare of your friends; but there is no blessing here without some alloy of grief, and such was to me the account of the poor state of dear Mrs. Wase's health. The Lord be with her, as a Comforter and Sanctifier, if He does not choose to be with her as a Physician. Tell her, I should be glad to hold up her hands in her fight of affliction, but if the poor, unprofitable, weak servant is far off, the Master, who is rich in mercy, who fills the whole world with His goodness and patience, who has all the power given Him, as "our Brother, Son of man," in heaven and earth—this kind Master is near to her and all His afflicted ones. Bid her from me, entreat her in my name, or rather in His dear name, Jesus, Salvation, Resurrection, Life, Light, and Love, to look to Him, and to make a free and constant use of Him, in all His offices.

I recommend to her two remedies: the one is a cheerful resignation to the will of God, whereby her animal spirits will be raised and sweetly refreshed;

the other is four lumps of heavenly sugar, to be taken every half hour, day and night, when she does not sleep. I make a constant use of them, to my great comfort. They have quickened my soul when I was dying, and I doubt not but they will have the same effect upon hers. Our Church has already extracted that divine sugar from the Scriptures, and put it into the Common Prayer-Book, as the heavenly bait, which is to draw us to the Lord's Table. Though they have often passed through my mouth, when I have called her there, they have lost nothing of their sweetness and force: "God so loved the world," etc.; "If any man sin," etc.; "It is a faithful saying," etc.; "Come unto Me all ye that are weary," etc. God grant her abundance of the faith which rolls these heavenly pills in the mind, and much of that love which sucks their sweetness in the heart. Tell her they go down best if taken in the cup of thankfulness, into which a tear of desire, of humility, of repentance, or of joy might be dropped occasionally. That tear is to be had by looking simply at Him who sells oil to the virgins, who offered a springing well to the woman of Samaria, and opened a fountain flowing with heavenly blood and water, when He hung for us upon the cross. To Him be praise and glory for ever. Amen.

From the "Life of Fletcher," by the Rev. J. Wesley.

To my very dear Friends and Benefactors, Charles and Mary Greenwood.

May 28, 1777.

My prayer shall always be that the merciful may find mercy, and that the great kindness I have found under your quiet roof may be shown you everywhere under the canopy of heaven. I think with grateful joy of the days of calm retreat I have been blest with at Newington, and lament my not having improved better the precious opportunities of sitting, Mary-like, at the feet of my great Physician. May He requite your kind care of a dying worm, by abundantly caring for you and yours, and making all your bed in your sickness! May you enjoy full health! May you hunger and thirst after righteousness, and be abundantly filled therewith! May you sweetly rest in Christ! May His protection be as a wall of fire round about you and yours! May His rod and His staff comfort you under all the troubles of life, the decay of the body, the assaults of the enemy, and the pangs of death! May you stand in the clefts of the Rock of Ages, and be safely sheltered there when all the storms of justice blow around! And may you always have such spiritual and temporal friends, helps, and comforts, as I have found in your pleasing retreat. You have received a poor Lazarus, you have had compassion like the good Samaritan; you have admitted me to the enjoyment of your best things; and now what can I say? What but "thanks be to God for His unspeakable gift"; and thanks to my dear friends for all their favours? They will, I trust, be found faithfully recorded in my breast, when the great Rewarder of them that diligently seek Him will render to every man according to his works. And a raised Lazarus shall then appear in the gate, to testify of the love of Charles and Mary Greenwood. I was a little better, but I now spit blood more than I had done for weeks before. Glory be to God for every providence! His will be done in me, by health or sickness, life or death. All from Him is, and I trust will be, welcome.

To a Friend.

1776.

I thank God I am not afraid of any evil tidings; my heart standeth fast, believing in the Lord, and desiring Him to do with me just whatever pleases Him. With respect to my body, my physician hopes I shall do well. And so I hope, and believe too. For health or sickness, life or death, is but when the Lord sends it. I am in hopes of seeing you soon. I am forbid preaching, but, blessed be God, I am not forbidden by my heavenly Physician to pray, believe, and love. This is a sweet work which heals, strengthens, and delights; let us do it till we have recovered our spiritual strength. And then, whether we shall be seen on earth or not, it will be all alike.

To a Friend.

1779.

Let us bear with patience the decays of nature, let us see without fear the approach of death. We must put off this sickly, corruptible body, in order to put on the immortal and glorious garment. I have some hopes that my poor sister will yet be my sister in Christ. Her self-righteousness, I trust, breaks as fast as her body. I am come hither to see death make havoc among my friends. I wear mourning for my father's brother, and for my brother's son. The same mourning will serve me for my dying sister, if I do not go before her. She lies on the same bed where my father and mother died, and where she and I were born. How near is life to death! But, blessed be God, Christ the Resurrection is nearer to the weak, dying believer! Death works through the body, and the Resurrection through the soul. And our soul is our real self.

From a "Life of Fletcher," published in America.

To W. Smith, Esq.

November, 1783.

The many and great favours you have loaded us with during our long stay under your hospitable roof, prompted us to make the earliest acknowledgments of our obligations, and to beg you would receive our warmest thanks for such unexpected and undeserved tokens of brotherly love. . . . And now, sir, what shall we say? You are our generous benefactor, and we your affectionate, though unprofitable, servants. In one sense we are on a level with those to whom you show your charity in the streets; we can do nothing but pray for you, your dear partner, and yours. You kindly received us for Christ's sake; may God receive you freely for His sake also! You have borne with our infirmities; the Lord bear with yours also! You have let your servants serve us; the Lord give all His servants and His angels charge concerning you, that you hurt not your foot against a stone, and may you be helped out of every difficulty! You have given us a most pleasing resting-place, and comfortable apartments under your roof, and next your own chamber; the Lord grant you eternal rest with Him in His heavenly mansions! May He Himself be your habitation and resting-place for ever, and place you and yours with His own jewels in the choicest repository of precious things! You have fed us with the richest food; may the Giver of every perfect gift fit you for a place at His table, and make you rank there with Abraham, Isaac, and Jacob! You have given us wines; may you drink with Christ Himself the fruit of the vine new in your Father's kingdom! You have given us a rich provision for the way; when you cross the flood, the deep flood of death, may you find that your heavenly Lord has made such a rich provision of faith, righteousness, hope, and joy for you, that you may rejoice, triumph, and sing, while you leave your earthly friends to go home!

WILLIAM COWPER.

IV.

WILLIAM COWPER was born in 1731, and called to the bar in 1754. He was appointed Clerk to the House of Lords in 1763, but, difficulties occurring about the appointment, insanity came on, from which he did not recover till 1765. He afterwards lived, with his friend, Mrs. Unwin, first at Huntingdon, then at Olney, and East Dereham. He was troubled by some returns of insanity at intervals. Most of his poetry was written at Olney. He died in 1800.

To Lady Hesketh.

July, 1765.

Since the visit you were so kind as to pay me in the temple, what have I not suffered! And since it has pleased God to restore to me the use of my reason, what have I not enjoyed! You know by experience how pleasant it is to feel the first approaches of health after a fever; but oh! the fever of the brain! To feel the quenching of that fire is indeed a blessing which I think it impossible to receive without the most consummate gratitude. Terrible as this chastisement is, I acknowledge in it the hand of an infinite justice; nor is it at all more difficult for me to perceive in it the hand of an infinite mercy likewise. When I consider the effect it has had upon me, I am exceedingly thankful for it, and, without hypocrisy, esteem it the greatest blessing, next to life itself, I ever received from the divine bounty. I pray God that I may ever retain this sense of it, and then I am sure I shall continue to be, as I am at present, really happy. . . . My affliction has taught me a road to happiness which, without it, I should never have found; and I know, and have experience of it every day, that the mercy of God, to him who believes himself to be the object of it, is more than sufficient to compensate for the loss of every other blessing.

To Mrs. Cowper, his Cousin.

April 4, 1766.

I have so much cause for humility, and so much need of it too, and every little sneaking resentment is such an enemy to it, that I hope I shall never give quarter to anything that appears in the shape of sullenness, or self-consequence hereafter. Alas! if my best Friend, who laid down His life for me, were to remember all the instances in which I have neglected Him, and to plead them against me in judgment, where should I hide my guilty head in the day of recompense? I will pray, therefore, for blessings on my friends, even though they cease to be so, and upon my enemies, though they continue such. The deceitfulness of the natural heart is inconceivable. I know well that I passed among my friends for a person at least religiously inclined, if not actually religious; and, what is more wonderful,

I thought myself a Christian, when I had no faith in Christ, when I saw no beauty in Him that I should desire Him; in short, when I had neither faith nor love, nor any Christian grace whatever, but a thousand seeds of rebellion instead, evermore springing up in enmity against Him. But blessed be God, even the God who is become my salvation, the hail of affliction and rebuke for sin has swept away the refuge of lies. It pleased the Almighty in great mercy to set all my misdeeds before me. At length, the storm being past, a quiet and peaceful serenity of soul succeeded, such as ever attends the gift of lively faith in the all-sufficient atonement, and the sweet sense of mercy and pardon purchased by the blood of Christ. Thus did He break me and bind me up, thus did He wound me and His hands made me whole.

To the Same.

September, 1766.

I am not sorry that what I have said concerning our knowledge of each other in a future state, has a little inclined you to the affirmative. For though the redeemed of the Lord shall be sure of being as happy in that state as infinite power, employed by infinite goodness, can make them, and therefore it may seem immaterial whether we shall, or shall not, recollect each other hereafter; yet our present happiness at least is a little interested in the question. A parent, a friend, a wife, must, I think, needs feel a little heart-ache at the thought of an eternal separation from the objects of her regard; and not to know them when she meets them in another life, or never to meet them at all, amounts, though not altogether, yet nearly, to the same thing. Remember them I think she needs must. To hear that they are happy will, indeed, be no small addition to her own felicity; but to see them will surely be a greater. . . . For my own part, this life is such a momentary thing, and all its interests have so shrunk in my estimation, since, by the grace of our Lord Jesus Christ, I became attentive to the things of another, that, like a worm in the bud of all my friendships and affections, this very thought would eat out the heart of them all, had I a thousand; and were their date to terminate with this life I think I should have no inclination to cultivate and improve such a fugitive business. Yet friendship is necessary to our happiness here; and, built upon Christian principles, upon which alone it can stand, is a thing even of religious sanction, for what is that love which the Holy Spirit, speaking by St. John, so much inculcates, but friendship?—the only love which deserves the name, a love which can toil, and watch, and deny itself, and go to death for its brother.

To Lady Hesketh.

March 6, 1766.

I have for some time past imputed your silence to the cause which you yourself assign for it, viz., to my change of situation; and was even sagacious enough to account for the frequency of your letters to me while I lived alone, from your attention to me in a state of such solitude as seemed to make it an act of particular charity to write to me. I blessed God for it—I was happy even then; solitude has nothing gloomy in it if the soul points upwards. St. Paul tells his Hebrew converts, "Ye are come (already come) to Mount Sion, to an innumerable company of angels, to the general assembly of the firstborn, which are written in heaven, and to Jesus, the mediator of the new covenant." When this is the case, as surely it was with them, or the Spirit of Truth had never spoken it, there is an end of the melancholy and dullness of life at once. You will not suspect me, my dear cousin, of a design to understand this passage literally. But this, however, it certainly means, that a lively faith is able, in some measure, to anticipate the joys of that heavenly society which the soul shall actually possess hereafter.

Since I have changed my situation I have found still greater cause of thanksgiving to the Father of all mercies. The family with whom I live are Christians; and it has pleased the Almighty to bring me to the knowledge of them, that I may want no means of improvement in that temper and conduct which He is pleased to require in all His servants. My dear cousin, one half of the Christian world would call this madness, fanaticism, and folly; but are not these things warranted by the

Word of God, not only in the passage I have cited, but in many others? If we have no communion with God here, surely we can expect none hereafter. A faith that does not place our conversation in heaven, that does not warm the heart and purify it too; that does not, in short, govern our thought, word, and deed, is no faith, nor will it obtain for us any spiritual blessing hereafter. Let us see, therefore, my dear cousin, that we do not deceive ourselves in a matter of such infinite moment. The world will be ever telling us that we are good enough; and the world will vilify us behind our backs. But it is not the world which tries the heart, that is the prerogative of God alone. My dear cousin, I have often prayed for you behind your back, and now I pray for you to your face. There are many who would not forgive me this wrong; but I have known you so long and so well, that I am not afraid of telling you how sincerely I wish for your growth in every Christian grace, in everything that may promote and secure your everlasting welfare.

To the Rev. J. Newton.

August 6, 1785.

God knows that, my mind having been occupied more than twelve years in the contemplation of the most distressing subjects, the world and its opinion of what I write has become as unimportant to me as the whistling of a bird in a bush. Despair made amusement necessary, and I found poetry the most agreeable amusement. Had I not endeavoured to perform my best, it would not have amused me at all. The mere blotting of so much paper would have been but indifferent sport. God gave me grace also to wish that I might not write in vain. Accordingly I have mingled much truth with much trifle; and such truths as deserved, at least, to be clad as well and as handsomely as I could clothe them. If the world approves me not, so much the worse for them, but not for me. I have only endeavoured to serve them, and the loss will be their own. And as to their commendations, if I should chance to win them, I feel myself equally invulnerable there. The view that I have had of myself for many years, has been so truly humiliating, that I think the praises of all mankind could not hurt me. God knows that I speak my present sense of the matter at least most truly, when I say that the admiration of creatures like myself seems to me a weapon the least dangerous that my worst enemy could employ against me. I am fortified against it by such solidity of real self-abasement, that I deceive myself most egregiously if I do not heartily despise it. Praise belongeth to God, and I seem to myself to covet it no more that I covet divine honours. Could I assuredly hope that God would at last deliver me, I should have reason to thank Him for all I have suffered, were it only for the sake of this single fruit of my affliction—that it has taught me how much more contemptible I am in myself than I ever before suspected, and has reduced my former share

F

of self-knowledge (of which at that time I had a tolerably good opinion) to a mere nullity in comparison with what I have acquired since. Self is a subject of inscrutable misery and mischief, and can never be studied to so much advantage as in the dark; for as the bright beams of the sun seem to impart a beauty to the foulest objects, and can make even a dunghill smile, so the light of God's countenance, vouchsafed to a fellow-creature, so sweetens and softens him for the time, that he seems, both to others and to himself, to have nothing savage or sordid about him. But the heart is a nest of serpents, and will be such while it continues to beat. If God cover the mouth of that nest with His hand, they are quiet and harmless; but if He withdraw His hand, the whole family lift up their heads and hiss, and are as active and venomous as ever. This I always professed to believe from the time that I had embraced the truth, but never knew it as I know it now. To what end I have been made to know it as I do, whether for the benefit of others, or for my own, or for both, or for neither, will appear hereafter.

To the Rev. William Unwin.

September 7, 1783.

Till the Incarnation of the Godhead is verily believed, He is unapproachable by man upon any terms; and in that case to accost Him as if we had a right of relationship, when in reality we have none, would be to affront Him to His face. But an Incarnate God is as much human as divine. When He assumed man's nature He revealed Himself as the Friend of man, as the Brother of every soul that loves Him. He conversed freely with man while He was upon the earth, and as freely with him after His resurrection. I doubt not, therefore, that it is possible, even now, to enjoy an access to Him unaccompanied with ceremonious awe, easy, delightful, and without constraint. This, however, can only be the lot of those who make it the business of their lives to please Him, and to cultivate communion with Him. And then, I presume, there can be no danger of offence, because such a habit of soul is of His own creation, and, near as we come, we come no nearer to Him than He is pleased to draw us. If we address Him as children, it is because He tells us He is our Father. If we unbosom ourselves to Him as a friend, it is because He calls us friends; and if we speak to Him in the language of love, it is because He first used it, thereby teaching us that it is the language He delights to hear from His people. But I confess that through the weakness, the folly, and corruption of human nature, this privilege, like all other Christian privileges, is liable to abuse. There is a mixture of evil in everything we do; indulgence encourages us to encroach, and while we exercise the rights of children, we become childish.

To the Same.

I say Amen, with all my heart, to your observation on religious characters. Men who profess themselves adepts in mathematical knowledge, in astronomy, or jurisprudence, are generally as well qualified as they would appear. The reason may be, that they are always liable to detection, should they attempt to impose upon mankind, and, therefore, take care to be what they pretend. In religion alone a profession is often lightly taken up and slovenly carried on, because, forsooth, candour and charity require us to hope the best, and to judge favourably of our neighbour, and because it is easy to deceive the ignorant, who are a great majority upon this subject. Let a man attach himself to a particular party, contend furiously for what are properly called Evangelical doctrines, and enlist himself under the banner of some popular preacher, and the business is done. Behold a Christian! a saint! a phœnix! In the mean time, perhaps, his heart and his temper, and even his conduct, are unsanctified, possibly less exemplary than those of some avowed infidels. No matter; he can talk, he has the shibboleth of the true Church, the Bible in his pocket, and a head well stored with notions. But the quiet, humble, modest person, who is in his practice what the other is only in his profession, who hates a noise, and therefore makes none; who, knowing the snares that are in the world, keeps himself as much out of it as he can, and never enters it but when duty calls, and even then with fear and trembling, is the Christian that will always stand highest in the estimation of those who bring all characters to the test of true wisdom, and judge of the tree by its fruit.

To the Rev. J. Newton.

No man was ever scolded out of his sins. The heart, corrupt as it is, and because it is so, grows angry if it be not treated with some management and good manners, and scolds again. A surly mastiff will bear, perhaps, to be stroked, though he will growl under that operation, but if you touch him roughly, he will bite. There is no grace that the spirit of self can counterfeit with more success than a religious zeal. A man thinks he is fighting for Christ, and he is fighting for his own notions. He thinks that he is skilfully searching the heart of others, when he is only gratifying the malignity of his own, and charitably supposes his hearers destitute of all grace, that he may shine the more in his own eyes by comparison. When he has performed this notable task, he wonders that they are not converted. "He has given it them soundly," and if they do not tremble and confess that God is in him, in truth he gives them up as reprobate, incorrigible, and lost for ever. But a man that loves me, if he sees me in an error, will pity me, and endeavour calmly to convince me of it, and persuade me to forsake it. If he has great and good news to tell me, he will not do it angrily, and in much heat and discomposure of spirit.

Olney, November, 1784.

My dear Friend,

To condole with you on the death of a mother, aged eighty-seven, would be absurd—rather, therefore, as is reasonable, I congratulate you on the almost singular felicity of having enjoyed the company of so amiable and so near a relation so long. Your lot and mine, in this respect, have been very different, as, indeed, in almost every other. Your mother lived to see you rise, at least to see you comfortably established in the world. Mine, dying when I was six years old, did not live to see me sink in it. You may remember with pleasure while you live a blessing vouchsafed to you so long, and I, while I live, must regret a comfort of which I was deprived so early. I can truly say that not a week passes (perhaps I might, with equal veracity, say a day), in which I do not think of her. Such was the impression her tenderness made upon me, though the opportunity she had for showing it was so short. But the ways of God are equal; and when I reflect on the pangs she would have suffered, had she been a witness of all mine, I see more cause to rejoice than to mourn that she was hidden in the grave so soon.

To the Rev. J. Newton.

Olney, May, 1785.

I am sensible of the tenderness and affectionate kindness with which you recollect our past intercourse, and express your hopes of my future restoration. I, too, within the last eight months have had my hopes, though they have been of short duration, cut off like the foam upon the waters. Some previous adjustments, indeed, are necessary, before a lasting expectation of comfort can have place in me. There are those persuasions in my mind, which either entirely forbid the entrance of hope, or, if it enter, immediately eject it. They are incompatible with any such inmate, and must be turned out themselves before so desirable a guest can have secure possession. This, you say, will be done. It may be, but it is not done yet; nor has a single step in the course of God's dealings with me been taken towards it. If I mend, no creature ever mended so slowly that recovered at last. I am like a slug or snail, that has fallen into a deep well; slug as he is, he performs his descent with an alacrity proportioned to his weight; but he does not crawl up again quite so fast. Mine was a rapid plunge; but my return to daylight, if I am indeed returning, is leisurely enough. I wish you a swift progress and a pleasant one through the great subject that you have in hand; and set that value upon your letters to which they are in themselves entitled, but which is certainly increased by that peculiar attention which the writer of them pays to me. Were I such as I once was, I should say that I have a claim upon your particular notice which nothing ought to supersede. Most of your other connections you may fairly be said to have formed by your own act; but your connection with me was the work of God. The kine that went up with the ark from Bethshemesh left what they loved behind them, in obedience to an impression which to them was perfectly dark and unintelligible. Your journey to Huntingdon was not less wonderful. He, indeed, who sent you, knew well wherefore, but you knew not. That dispensation, therefore, would furnish me, as long as we can both remember it, with a plea for some distinction at your hands, had I occasion to use and urge it, which I have not. But I am altered since that time; and if your affection for me had ceased, you might very reasonably justify your change by mine. I can say nothing for myself at present; but this I can venture to foretell, that, should the restoration of which my friends assure me obtain, I shall undoubtedly love those who have continued to love me, even in a state of transformation from my former self, much more than ever. I doubt not that Nebuchadnezzar had friends in his prosperity—all kings have many; but when his nails became like eagles' claws, and he ate grass like an ox, I suppose he had few to pity him.

To the Same.

Weston, January 13, 1787.

My dear Friend,

It gave me pleasure, such as it was, to learn from a letter to Mr. H. Thornton, that the inscription for the tomb of poor Unwin has been approved of—the dead having nothing to do with human praises; but if they died in the Lord, they have abundant praises to render to Him, which is far better. The dead, whatever they leave behind them, have nothing to regret. Good Christians are the only creatures in the world that are truly good, and them they will see again, and see them improved; therefore them they regret not. Regret is for the living. What we get, we soon lose, and what we lose we regret. The most obvious consolation in this case seems to be, that we who regret others shall quickly become objects of regret ourselves; for mankind are continually passing off in a rapid succession. I have many kind friends, who, like yourself, wish that instead of turning my endeavours to a translation of Homer, I had proceeded in the way of original poetry. But I can truly say that it was ordered otherwise, not by me, but by the Providence that governs all my thoughts, and directs my intentions as He pleases. It may seem strange, but it is true, that, after having written a volume, in general with great ease to myself, I found it impossible to write another page. The mind of man is not a fountain, but a cistern; and mine, God knows, a broken one. It is my creed that the intellect depends as much, both for the energy and the multitude of its exertions, upon the operations of God's agency upon it, as the heart, for the exercises of its graces, upon the influence of the Holy Spirit. According to this persuasion, I may very reasonably affirm that it was not God's pleasure that I should proceed in the same task, because He did not enable me to do it. A whole year I waited, and waited in circumstances of mind that made a state of non-employment peculiarly irksome to me. I longed for the pen as the only remedy, but I could find no subject. Extreme distress of spirit at last drove me, as, if I mistake not, I told you some time since, to lay Homer before me, and translate for amusement. Why it pleased God that I should be hunted into such a business of such enormous length and labour, by miseries for which He did not see good to afford me any other remedy, I know not. But so it was; and jejune as the consolation may be, and unsuited to the exigencies of a mind that once was spiritual, yet a thousand times have I been glad of it; for a thousand times it has saved me, at least to divert my attention, in some degree, from such terrible tempests as I believe have seldom been permitted to beat upon a human mind. Let my friends, therefore, who wish me some little measure of tranquility in the performance of the most turbulent voyage that ever Christian mariner made, be contented, that, having Homer's mountains and forests to windward, I escape, under their shelter, from the force of many a gust that would almost overset me; especially when they consider that, not by choice, but by necessity, I make them my refuge. As to fame and honour and glory, they may be acquired by poetical feats of any sort. God knows that if I could lay me down in my grave with hope at my side, or sit with hope at my side in a dungeon all the residue of my days, I would cheerfully waive them all; for the little fame that I have already earned has never saved me from one distressing night, or from one despairing day, since I first acquired it. For what I am reserved, or to what, is a mystery; I would fain hope, not merely that I may amuse others, or only be a translator of Homer.

To SAMUEL ROSE, ESQ.

Weston, June 23, 1788.

It has pleased God to give us rain, without which this part of the country at least must soon have become a desert. The meadows have been parched to a January brown; and we have foddered our cattle for some time, as in the winter. The goodness and power of God are never, I believe, so universally acknowledged as at the end of a long drought. Man is naturally a self-sufficient animal, and, in all concerns that seem to lie within the sphere of his own ability, thinks little or not at all of the need he always has of protection and furtherance from above. But he is sensible that the clouds will not assemble at his bidding, and that, though the clouds assemble, they will not fall in showers because he commands them. When, therefore, at last the blessing descends, you shall hear even in the streets the most irreligious and thoughtless with one voice exclaim, "Thank God!" confessing themselves indebted to His favour, and willing, at least so far as words go, to give Him the glory. I can hardly doubt, therefore, that the earth is sometimes parched, and the crops endangered, in order that the multitude may not want a memento to whom they owe them, nor absolutely forget the power on which all depend for all things.

To the Rev. J. Newton.

The Lodge, December 5, 1720.

My dear Friend,

Sometimes I am too sad and sometimes too busy to write; both these causes have concurred lately to keep me silent. But more than by either of these, I have been hindered since I received your last by a violent cold, which oppressed me during almost the whole month of November. Your letter affects us with both joy and sorrow; with sorrow and sympathy respecting poor Mrs. Newton, whose feeble and dying state suggests a wish for her release, rather than for her continuance; and joy on your account, who are enabled to bear, with so much resignation and cheerful acquiescence in the will of God, the prospect of a loss, which even they who know you best apprehended might prove too much for you. As to Mrs. Newton's interest in the best things, none, intimately acquainted with her as we have been, could doubt it. She doubted it indeed, herself; but though it is not our duty to doubt any more than it is our privilege, I have always considered the self-condemning spirit, to which such doubts are principally owing, as one of the most favourable symptoms of a nature spiritually renewed, and have many a time heard you make the same observation. We believe that the best Christian is occasionally subject to doubts and fears, and that they form a part of the great warfare. That it is our privilege and duty to cultivate an habitual sense of peace in the conscience, and that this peace will be enjoyed in proportion as faith is in exercise, and the soul is in communion with God, we fully agree. But who that is acquainted with the inward experience of the Christian, does not know that there are alternations of joy, and fear, of triumph, and of depression? The Psalms of David furnish many instances of this fact, as well as the history of the most eminent saints recorded in Scripture, "Though I am sometime afraid, yet put I my trust in Thee." We conceive these words to be an exemplification of the truth of the case. When, therefore, we hear persons speak of the entire absence of sin and infirmity, and exemption from doubts and fears, we are strongly disposed to believe that they labour under great self-deception, and know little of their own hearts in thus arguing against the general testimony of the Church of

Christ in all ages. A plain and pious Christian once told us of an appropriate remark that he addressed to an individual who professed to be wholly free from any fears on this subject. "If," observed this excellent man, "you have no fears for yourself, you must allow me to entertain some for you."

To WILLIAM HAYLEY, ESQ.

Weston, January 29, 1793.

MY DEAREST HAYLEY,

I truly sympathize with you under your weight of sorrow for the loss of our good Samaritan. But be not broken-hearted, my friend! Remember the loss of those we love is the condition on which we live ourselves; and that he who chooses his friends wisely from among the excellent of the earth, has a sure ground to hope concerning them when they die, that a merciful God has made them far happier than they could be here, and that we shall join them soon again. This is solid comfort, could we but avail ourselves of it; but I confess the difficulty of doing so. Sorrow is like the deaf adder, "that hears not the voice of the charmer, charm he never so wisely;" and I feel so much myself for the death of Austen, that my own chief consolation is, that I had never seen him. Live yourself, I beseech, for I have seen so much of you that I can by no means spare you, and I will live as long as it shall please God to permit. I know you set some value on me, therefore let that promise comfort you, and give us not reason to say, like David's servant, "We know that it would have pleased thee more if all we had died, than this one, for whom thou art inconsolable." You have still Romney, and Carwardine, and Guy, and me, and my poor Mary, and I know not how many beside; as many, I suppose, as ever had an opportunity of spending a day with you. He who has the most friends must necessarily lose the most, and he whose friends are numerous as yours may the better spare a part of them. It is a changing, transient scene! yet a little while, and this poor dream of life will be over with all of us. The living, and they who live unhappy, they are indeed subjects of sorrow.

Adieu, my beloved friend.

Ever yours,
W. C.

HANNAH MORE.

V.

HANNAH MORE was born in 1745. She showed her great powers of mind in early life, and when about thirty years of age she made considerable mark in the literary world. In 1785 she went to live at Cowslip Green, near Bristol, from which she afterwards moved to Barley Wood. In 1789 she was struck with the wretched condition of the people in and around Cheddar, and devoted herself to establishing schools and other means of instruction. So far as health permitted, she continued her good work till the end of her life, in 1833.

TO THE REV. JOHN NEWTON.

Cowslip Green, July 23, 1778.

As I have observed to you before, so much do my gardening cares and pleasures occupy me, that the world is not half so formidable a rival to heaven, in my heart, as my garden. I trifle away more time than I ought, under pretence (for I must have a creditable motive to impose even upon myself) that it is good for my health; but in reality because it promises a sort of indolent pleasure, and keeps me from thinking and finding out what is amiss in myself. The world, though I live in the gay part of it, I do not actually love, yet friendship and kindness have combined to fix me there, and I dearly love many individuals in it. When I am in the great world, I consider myself as in an enemy's country, and as beset with snares, and this puts me on my guard. I know that many people, whom I hear say a thousand brilliant and agreeable things, disbelieve, or at least disregard, those truths on which I found my everlasting hopes. This sets me upon a more diligent inquiry into those truths, and "upon the arch of Christianity the more I press the stronger I find it." Fears and snares seem necessary to excite my circumspection, for it is certain that my mind has more langour, and my faith less energy here, where I have no temptations from without, and where I live in the full enjoyment and constant perusal of the most beautiful objects of inanimate nature—the lovely wonders of the munificence and bounty of God. Yet in the midst of His blessings, I should be yet more tempted to forget Him, were it not for the frequent nervous headaches and low fevers which I feel to be wonderfully wholesome for my moral health. I feel grateful, dear sir, for your kind anxiety for my best interests. My situation is, as you rightly apprehend, full of danger; yet less from the pleasures than from the deceitful favour and the insinuating applause of the world. The goodness of God will, I humbly trust, preserve me from taking up with so poor a portion—nay, I hope that what He has given me is to show that all is nothing short of Himself; yet there are times when I am tempted to think it a great deal, and to forget Him who has promised to be my portion for ever.

CHARLES SIMEON.

VI.

CHARLES SIMEON was born in 1758, ordained in 1782, appointed to Trinity Church, Cambridge, 1783, Vice-Provost of King's College, Cambridge, 1792, died November 13, 1836.

To one of his greatest Friends.
1786.

Twice have I begun to write to you, but neither time had an opportunity of proceeding very far; once being interrupted by my father, and the other time by some other avocation. Though I have not answered your letter for so long a season, I think I may say that I have scarcely ever been enabled to pray for myself but I have prayed also for you, because you are deeply engraven on my heart, and I long for the establishment of your body in health, and your soul in grace. Mr. Atkinson, who loves you dearly, rather rejoiced in hearing of your trials, because they would tend to divest you of all high thoughts of yourself, and make you live more by faith on our dear Redeemer. Certain it is that the saints whom God has most approved have been most abundantly exercised in different manners for the trial of their faith; and they who are most earnest in prayer for grace are often most afflicted, because the graces which they pray for—faith, hope, patience, humility, are only to be wrought in us by means of these trials, which call forth the several graces into act and exercise; and in the very exercise of them they are all strengthened and confirmed. May this be your blessed experience and mine. I desire to thank you most sincerely for your kind observations, respecting misguided zeal, and my danger from that quarter. Such observations were not only necessary then, but are so every day, as I find by frequent experience. That which is characteristic of a man's disposition, and is his besetting sin in a state of nature, will most generally remain so when he is in a state of grace, with this difference only, that in the former case it has the entire ascendant over him, in the latter it meets with continual checks, and is not suffered to have dominion. It is promised that "if we walk in the Spirit, we shall not fulfil the lusts of the flesh," but not that we shall find no temptations to fulfil them.

To Another Friend.

1798.

The only excuse I can make for my neglect is, that my attention to my work is so unintermittent as to leave me no time to see a friend, to write a letter. . . . You will say I overdo the matter, and shall hurt my health. I answer, I trust not, because I make a point of riding every day, unless my work or the weather make it particularly inconvenient. Blessed be God, my work is my meat and drink; I only want more spirituality in it. Marvellous news have I to tell you of the goodness of God. Pride and vanity and unbelief would have been ready to suggest (but thanks be to God, who did not permit me to listen to them!) that if I went away for four months the work would be at a stand at home. Behold! since my return, no less than nineteen persons have applied to be received into my societies, of whom I had no knowledge at all when I went away; and what is wonderfully gracious, there is not one of them who owed his first impressions to my ministry, and but one to the ministry of Mr. Thomason. All were awakened, either gradually or insensibly, by God Himself, or by conversation with one or other of my people. Does not this say aloud in our ears that if we will endeavour to move in God's way, and do His work, He will take care of our concerns? So I construe it, and the reflection affords me infinitely more consolation than if I had been instrumental to their conversion.

To a Young Clergyman.

I greatly desire to hear from you: what reception you have met with; what trials you find; how you are enabled to withstand them; what is the frame of your mind; and whether, while you are "in weakness and fear and much trembling," you still find your soul increasingly strengthened to war a good warfare. For till I hear *from* you, I do not know what in particular to say *to* you; I can only speak in general terms. Doubtless I may judge in some measure of the feelings of your heart, by what I have so often felt in my own; that sometimes you seem determined to live for God, and for Him only; that at other times, through the influence of inward corruption or outward temptations, you seem to halt; and thus that you are maintaining a daily conflict. But if my dear friend will open his mind freely and fully, I will endeavour, with God's permission, to do the same on my part. . . . My dear friend, walk close with God—it is the only way to be either safe or happy; live retired; read much; pray much; abound in all offices of love; shun the company that may draw you aside; consider yourself as a soldier that is not to be entangled with the things of this life, in order that you may please Him who has chosen you to be a soldier; finally, be faithful unto death, and Christ will give you a crown of life.

A Private Letter, putting an End to a Controversy in Print.

Permit me to return you my best thanks for the present of your remarks, and to say that I most cordially agree with you in terminating our public correspondence. I hope the desire of both of us is to do all the good we can while we are here, and to obtain, both for ourselves and others, eternal happiness hereafter; and I am persuaded that if circumstances should ever bring us into a nearer acquaintance with each other, we should find that the difference between us, though certainly great, is not so great as may at first sight appear. . . . The number of those who are zealous in the cause of religion is not so great but that they may find ample scope for their exertions, without wasting their time in mutual contentions, and it is my earnest wish that the only strife we may ever know in future may be that which the apostles recommend of "contending earnestly for the faith once delivered to the saints," and of "provoking one another to love and to good works."

To Mr. Thomason.

1812.

What a treasure is that letter of Mr. Martyn to Mr. Corrie! It affords just such a view of our beloved friend as I would have wished to see. When we have nothing to call forth particular feelings, we go on in the common jog-trot way; but on such an occasion as that, the heart shows itself in its true light, and there is in that letter an artless simplicity which I must admire. As for sitting down to write a religious letter, it is what I cannot do myself, and what I do not very much admire unless there be some particular occasion that calls for it. I love rather that a letter be a free and easy communication of such things as are upon the mind, and such as we imagine will interest the person with whom we correspond. Some, indeed, who have a talent for letter writing, may employ their pen profitably in the more direct and formal way; but it is a thing I cannot do; religion with me is only the salt with which I season the different subjects on which I write; and it is recommended by St. Paul to be used in the whole of our converse with each other. Doubtless, when the mind can soar, and we can dip our pen in angels' ink, it is most delightful to prosecute the heavenly theme; but to sit down in cold blood and say, "I must now write a religious letter," is to me an irksome task, which I leave to those who have talents for it. In a word, religious communications are then most delightful when they proceed from the abundance of the heart; but all the sweetness of them is taken away when they are constrained and formal.

To a Friend.

December 10, 1817.

My dear Friend,

I should be cautious of making up my mind *strongly* on anything that is not clearly defined in Holy Scripture. Nothing is easier than to lay down an apparently good principle, and to err in following it; *e.g.*, the eating of meat offered to idols. Do not make bonds for your own feet; constructed as your mind is, you will be in danger of this. In things that are good and evil *per se*, there is no room for expediency; in things that are good or evil only *by accident,* expediency must guide you. Many think that the opposite to right must be wrong; but the opposite to right may be right, as in the instance before specified. . . . The human mind is very fond of fetters, and is apt to forge them for itself.

To Miss Gurney.

March 30, 1821.

I often think that my mind is very peculiarly constructed in this respect, that the death of those who are dear to me is in many cases a real source of joy, from a realizing view which I have of their happiness. But a few days ago a relation of Mr. Scott was regretting that he was drawing near his closing scene; and so far was I from sympathizing with him in this regret, that I could not refrain from congratulating the departing saint on his prospects. I say the same in reference to dear Priscilla. Had she been restored to health and usefulness in the Church, I should have regarded that as a source of unspeakable joy; but to have her kept here in a state of extreme langour, without any prospect of ever rendering any further services to the Church, would have been in my mind rather a matter of submission, than of desire. Of her preparation for glory no one can entertain a shadow of a doubt; why then keep her from it? Why not rejoice in her full possession of it? Why not consider her as just gone a stage before us, and redouble our own speed to enjoy her society again, as soon as we may be permitted to arrive at those blessed abodes? Yet whilst I say this I mean not that the feelings of nature should be suppressed, but sanctified and elevated to a heavenly refinement. And I feel assured that such will be the one sentiment that will pervade you all, when assembled on the mournful occasion of committing her mortal remains to the tomb. I even now taste the spirit of you all; I seem to be one with you all; I think I understand you all, and you also understand me. I love the "gathering into stillness," the sweet sorrow, and the adoring joy. But I must restrain my pen, lest I should seem to forget that "Jesus wept." Yet methinks if I know a little what it is to rejoice with trembling, I know also what it is to be melted with love, and to rejoice with weeping.

To the Duchess of Beaufort.

May 13, 1829.

On the subject of your grace's letter I have always felt myself incompetent to advise those who move in the higher walks of life. I know, in a measure, what the blessed Word of God says in relation to our separation from the world, and I know, in a measure, the line of conduct that befits my own situation in life. . . . I am a man of some firmness and decision of character, and from the first moment that I set myself to seek the Lord, I gave myself wholly up to Him, and separated myself altogether from the world. I had no one to control me; my situation favoured it; the people about me had not, so far as

I could see, one particle of what I judged to be the only true wisdom; and therefore I walked with Him only who had chosen and called me to be His servant. And to this hour I have ever persevered in this course. I feel, and have ever felt, that I have no talents for the world, no taste for the world, no time for the world; and, therefore, except as an ambassador from the Lord, I have had for forty-four years almost as little to do with the world, as if I had not been in the world. It were, therefore, easy for me to draw my line broad, and to make as little distinction for others as I have made for myself. But it does not appear to me that this would consort either with wisdom or with love. . . . A person who views the subject broadly, and without reference to the different circumstances of men, finds it easy to adduce strong and sweeping expressions, and to require a full conformity to them, without any modification whatever. But one who takes into account all the varieties of situation in which Christians move, and all the diversities of circumstances under which they may be placed, will feel it his duty to consider what those situations and circumstances call for, and what influence they ought to have on the conduct of those who are found in them. They will be led to distinguish between the letter and the spirit of a command, and to worship the former, whilst in the strictest possible way they adhere to and require the latter. . . . In the habit of our mind we should be altogether dead to the world, but in our acts we are not so called upon to separate from all ungodly persons as to have no intercourse with them whatever; for then, as the apostle says, we must needs go out of the world, whereas our blessed Lord prayed, not that we should be taken out of the world, but be kept from the evil of it. . . . In my opinion, it is not by abandoning our situation in life that we are to honour God, but by being examples in it, and by filling it to His glory. . . . To shut ourselves up entirely from the world, and put our light under a bushel, is the more easy; but to be blameless and harmless as the sons of God, without rebuke in the midst of a crooked and perverse nation, shining among them as lights in the world, and holding forth among them the Word of God, is in my opinion more worthy of our profession, more honourable to our God, and more beneficial to those whose welfare we are bound to seek.

To a Friend who was suffering Persecution.

1825.

God is now calling you to serve Him and to honour Him in a more especial manner; and I trust you will approve yourself a good soldier of Jesus Christ. As for receding from the field of battle, I hope you will not entertain the thought for a single moment. The eyes of all the University will be fiexd on you; and by your conduct many will be either intimidated, or emboldened to maintain their holy profession with more firmness than ever. God is putting great honour upon you, in that He is making you a partaker of Christ's sufferings. The Spirit of glory and of God is now made more visibly to rest upon you. It is as a Christian, and for the name of Christ, that you are reproached; and, therefore, instead of being ashamed, you have reason to glorify God on this behalf. Your less enlightened friends will pity you, but those who are better instructed out of the Holy Scriptures will congratulate you. Moses possessed a higher situation than you did, and voluntarily resigned it all that he might "suffer affliction with the people of God." He balanced against each other *the best of this world—* all the riches of the greatest kingdom upon earth, and the *want of religion,* reproach, and the cross; and he found that the Christian's portion was a talent of gold against a feather. Seek from God the same faith as he possessed, and you will soon both approve his choice and follow his example. And who can tell what God has for you to do for the advancement of His kingdom? . . . But I would earnestly wish you not to be precipitate as to any measures which you shall adopt. God, who has called you to this trial, will make your way plain before your face, if only you wait upon Him in faith and patience. I did intend to have written you a long letter, but my pressing engagements have prevented me from executing my purpose. I would only add, What would Paul have said to you in existing circumstances? Would he have used the language of consolation? Would he not of congratulation rather? Yes, assuredly of congratulation, and I have no doubt but that "after you have suffered awhile," God will "stablish, strengthen, settle you," and turn all your troubles into occasions of praise and thanksgiving.

To Mrs. Cunningham, about a Memoir which she had sent him.

November 12, 1827.

This is the religion which I love. I love simplicity, I love contrition, I love affiance, I love the tender breathings of affection. Talkativeness and boasting are not at all to my mind; I am jealous of everything, that, even in appearance, savours of self. Even religion itself I do not love, if it be not cast in a mould of humility and contrition. I love the religion of heaven; to fall on our faces, whilst we adore the Lamb, is the kind of religion which my soul affects, and it was this spirit which I so admired in your beloved sister. . . . I am in the habit of accounting religion as the simplest of all concerns. "To Him that loved us, and washed us from our sins in His own blood, and hath made us kings and priests unto our God, to Him be glory and dominion for ever and ever," expresses the very frame of mind in which I wish both to live and die. In that dear departed saint I saw it all. It seemed to be the very spirit of her mind; it was her meat and drink; and soon, I trust, we shall join her in this blessed song. I greatly rejoice that so many of her family are likeminded with her, having their views of the

Saviour alike clear, and their feelings towards Him alike elevated. May you, my dear madam, and I also, drink more and more into her spirit.

To the Bishop of Calcutta.

May 22, 1832.

I do not wonder that all are desirous of seeing you before you go, and of obtaining from you a parting blessing. At my time of life I have no hope of seeing you again till we meet before the throne of our reconciled God and Father. It is, doubtless, a most joyful thought that we have redemption through the blood of our adorable Saviour, even the forgiveness of sins. But I have no less comfort in the thought that He is exalted to give *repentance* and remission of sins. I would not wish for the latter without the former. I scarcely ask for the latter in comparison with the former. I feel willing to leave the latter altogether in God's hands, if I may but obtain the former. Repentance is in every way so desirable, so necessary, so suited to honour God, that I seek *that* above all. The tender heart, the broken and contrite spirit, are to me far above all the joys that I could ever hope for in this vale of tears. I long to be in my proper place, my hand on my mouth, and my mouth in the dust. I would rather have my seed-time here, and wait for my harvest till I myself am carried to the granary of heaven. I feel this to be safe ground. Here I cannot err. If I have erred all my days, I cannot err here. I am sure that whatever God may despise (and I am afraid that there is much which passes under the notion of religious experience that will not stand very high in His estimation), He will not despise the broken and contrite heart. I love the picture of the heavenly hosts, both saints and angels; all of them are upon their faces before the throne. I love the cherubim, with their wings before their faces and their feet. I think we hardly set this forth in our sermons as we ought to do. At all events, for *me*, I feel that this is the proper posture now, and will be to all eternity. But I am running on further than I like to do on such *interior* subjects; and am giving you, ere I am aware of it, my parting, dying testimony.

To the Same.

May 21, 1834.

About six weeks ago I sent to your son, to entreat that he would write to inform you why you had not heard from me in answer to your letter received about the beginning of February. At that time I was attacked with the gout. . . . My pains, after the first three weeks, were, through the tender mercy of God, scarcely worth a thought; but my whole frame was reduced to a perfect skeleton; and repeatedly was I considered as at the point of death. On this day three weeks I was reported, and not without reason, as dead. . . . You will ask me, perhaps, what was my frame of mind during this nearness to the eternal world. And I am happy to say that I found my principles quite able to sustain me. I have taught others that there is not so much as a sparrow that falls to the ground without our heavenly Father's special appointment, nor any one thing which shall not work for the good of His chosen people; and these things I was enabled so to realize as to have my soul kept in perfect peace. Throughout the whole time I was strengthened to rest on God as my covenant God and Father, and to believe that His covenant was ordered in all things and sure. The time, the measure, the duration of my illness were all in His hands; and I was content, yea thankful, yea joyful, to leave them there, and to wait His will, whatever it might be. As for joyful anticipations of the blessedness of heaven, neither the habit of my mind, nor the state of my body, nor, indeed, the character of my religion (the religion of a sinner at the foot of the cross) led to them; to be kept in perfect peace was more in accordance with my wishes, and that mercy God richly vouchsafed unto me; and I hope that if restored to any measure of health and strength, I shall be enabled more than ever to live for God, and to the glory of His great name. I am not fond of talking of self, but I have thought that to say thus much was due to you. . . . In a word, I felt, and do feel, that in God, and in God alone, I have all that I can need, and therefore my eyes are turned to Him always—Him exclusively —Him without a shadow of a doubt. Were I to look at Him through the medium of my own experience, it would be like looking at the sun through the medium of the waters—the sun in that case would appear to move as the water undulates; whereas, when viewed by Himself alone, He is uniformly and steadily the same, without any variableness or shadow of turning.

To Miss Elliott.

May 21, 1834.

I could not but weep over your kind and affectionate letter, insomuch that my constant attendant said to me, "Sir, I fear you have had some bad news to-day." I thank you most tenderly for all the expressions of your love, of which, alas! I feel myself most unworthy. You evidently do not know my state; it is that of a poor sinner before God; it is that which I ever expected it to be; and, in fact, ever wished it to be. Any other would be utterly unsuited to my whole life. . . . Of course you will not understand me as saying that I do not wish to be more holy and heavenly, but simply that, seeing that I am what I am, I am willing, yea desirous, that God should be glorified in the salvation of the very chief of sinners. . . . If Job, after seeing God, as it were, with his eyes, abhorred himself and repented in dust and ashes, what frame can be so fit for *me?* Young persons, to whom reconciliation with God is quite a novelty, may have great ebullitions of joy; and others, who have a vivid imagination, may go up to heaven and behold all the glory of it, and join with the heavenly choir in their songs of praise. I have no imagination—I never had; plain, simple truth has been more in accordance with the natural construction of my mind, and more suited to my taste, and I am inclined to think that God deals with men in a way suited to their constitutional feelings and acquired habits. I do not, therefore, regret my want of devout and joyful anticipations, for I had peace without a moment's intermission, even the peace that passeth all understanding. But this I bitterly regret—a want of divine savour on my soul, a want of tenderness of spirit, a want of devout admiration and gratitude. These have solely a respect to *God*, as a part of adoration; but the anticipations of glory have more respect to *ourselves*, and the blessedness that awaits us. Therefore, as having less to do with the imagination and with self, I prefer the shame and confusion of face, which I am conscious my whole life calls for, and which is less open to delusion of any kind. Yet I do not condemn or despise the things which I lack. I can easily conceive them to be high manifestations of a meetness for heaven; but I am not grieved that they do not enter into, and much less characterize, my experience. I have often wished that there were more of holy reverence in religious people when speaking of God and of the things which He has wrought for their salvation. I see not an instance of any remarkable visitation of God to man, which did not instantly generate in his heart and produce in his act a lowly reverence and self-abasement, and

I cannot but think that the nearer we approach to the eternal world, the more that feeling should be wrought within us.

To the Same.

November 27, 1835.

In your letter of this morning, you express a fear that you may love your dear mother, or a friend, too much; and I am anxious to correct that idea without loss of time; first, because it is a source of disquiet to the conscience; and next, because it is an error which prevails in the Church of God. That we may show our love improperly I readily grant; but that we can love one another too much, I utterly deny, provided only it be in subserviency to the love of God. I think I have explained to you that word "*fervently*"—"see that ye love one another with a pure heart fervently"—its precise meaning is "*intensely*." No two words in any two languages more exactly agree than "intensely" does with the original. If, then, our love be with a pure heart, this alone were sufficient to establish the point. But I am anxious to convey to you more fully my views on this matter, because, as God Himself is Love, I think that the more intensely I love those who are beloved of Him, the more I think I resemble Him. The proper model for our love to each other is Christ's love for us. If you will not fall short of that, I have no fear of your exceeding it. We are required to lay down our lives for the brethren.

We shall not easily exceed that.... But see it in operation. We read of those who would have plucked out their own eyes, and given them for the apostle; yea, and who even laid down their own necks for the apostle. Was Epaphroditus carried to excess when he "disregarded his own life" to supply the lack of service of others towards the apostle? What shall we say, then, of the apostle himself, who counted the pouring out of his heart's blood like a libation upon the sacrifice of his people's faith, a ground of joy and a subject for congratulation? But here an apostle was in one case the object, and in the other case the subject, of this love; and therefore we can scarcely hope for such attainments as theirs. Then let us come to one more like ourselves, Jonathan, of whom David says, "Thy love to me was wonderful, passing the love of women." Now, whether we understand this of woman's love to man, or, as I understand it, of man's love to woman (for I have no conception of woman's love surpassing, or even equalling, man's to woman), it is spoken not with blame, but with commendation, and I would not that I, or any one whom I love, should fall short of that. "He loved David," we are told, "as he loved his own soul;" and we cannot easily go beyond that; yet is that the proper measure for a *friend*. Perhaps you will say, My grief is that my love generates disquietude when those who are dear to me are ill; and this is an evidence that my love is idolatrous, and not truly Christian. Then what will you say to Paul, who confesses "he had no rest in his spirit because he found not Titus his brother"? Christianity does not encourage apathy; it is to regulate, not to eradicate our affections. It admits of their full operation, but tempers them in their measure and sanctifies them to the Lord. I have often been comforted in knowing that Lazarus and his sisters were peculiarly beloved of their Lord, and that John was an object of His more than ordinary attachment; and from hence you will see that if I have written this for your instruction, I have had an eye also to my own vindication.

To Dr. King.

February 6, 1836.

I thank God, who, in His tender mercy, has restored you to health both of body and mind. In all cases of affliction it is my habit to ask, "Whence came you? whither go you?" And the answer I invariably receive speedily and effectually composes my mind; "I come from your Father, to bring you into closer communion with Him, and richer knowledge of Him, and more entire conformity to His image." I apprehend this had been Paul's habit, when, in the midst of such afflictions as no other man ever sustained for so long a time, he cried in reference to them all, "I take pleasure." (See James i. 2.) I do not act thus in reference to the afflictions of my friends. There I would "weep with those that weep." But my sympathy relates to the present only; whilst faith and hope carry me on to the future, and enable me with a degree of comfort to anticipate "the end" (James v. 11). It has been thus as it respects you. First, I have said, where there is so much physical excitement, I do not wonder that there should be some physical depression. Perhaps, too, God may have sent the latter to reprove and correct the former. And I doubt not but that the effect will be to make the future elevation of your mind more pure and spiritual. Your religion has always been characterized by *life*. It may henceforth be of a deeper and more sombre character, like that in heaven, where they all prostrate themselves with deepest self-abasement, even whilst they sing their loudest songs. The finest melodies that were ever made have not only admitted of touches of the bass, or double-bass, but have by means of them been rendered incomparably more sublime. And I trust your melodies will, by means of your late afflictions, become more attuned to the melodies of heaven.

To a Person under Deep Mental Distress.

August 9, 1836.

You judge well; there is the same God now as formerly delivered Peter from prison in answer to the prayers of His people, and He is still a God that heareth prayer. I can in some small measure sympathize with you. I have known what it was to envy the dogs their mortality, and almost to wish them cursed with my immortality in my stead.

But I found God to be abundant both in mercy and truth, and so will you find Him, if, in the name of His dear Son, you wait patiently upon Him. With the desponding soul God justly expostulates (Isaiah xl. 27), and exposing the folly of such a state (ver. 28), gives us a clear direction for our deliverance, and a promise that shall surely be fulfilled to us in its season (ver. 29—31). I would have you, therefore, expostulate with your own soul, as David did (Psalm xlii. 11, and xliii. 5). That there is ground for humiliation in the best men, there is no doubt; holy Job exclaimed, "Behold, I am vile!" But to the vilest of men there is no ground for despondency when we recollect that the "blood of Jesus Christ cleanseth from all sin," and that He has said He would cast out *none* that came to Him. The Psalmist himself was in your state, and justly ascribed his despondency to his own weakness. He saw how erroneous had been all his conceptions of the Deity, and learned to look from Himself to the Holy Scriptures, in order to form a right judgment of His power of grace. Follow him in this respect, and you shall ere long follow him also in his testimony in behalf of God, as an Almighty and All-merciful Benefactor. I have no wish to know your name. It is sufficient for me that you are a fellow-sinner in distress. The Lord, even our great High Priest, has your name written on His breastplate, and *that* is my consolation when I am constrained, through forgetfulness, to express my intercessions generally; when, if I were able to spread before my

God the names and states of all for whom I have been asked to pray, I would gladly do so. I hope, with tender sympathy, to spread your case before Him, and I entreat the favour of you to remember before the throne of grace one, who, if he be not distressed like you, needs quite as much the prayers and intercessions of others on his behalf, even your faithful servant,

C. SIMEON.

To the Bishop of Calcutta, on the Indian Episcopate.

September 29, 1836.

Your most welcome letter has just arrived, and, though incapable of writing a syllable myself, I lose not a minute in answering it. Till within this week, I have been favoured with an energy, both of body and mind, far beyond what I could reasonably have looked forward to; and to give you some account of my visitation, for I am too proud to call it visit, I begin with that. To Cheltenham, Hereford, Darlaston, Newcastle-under-Lyne, and Derby. I have been on a visit to the different ministers appointed there by me; and such a continuation of love, during the whole eight weeks of my visit, has really far exceeded what I had supposed possible in this fallen world. My efforts in every place, both in public and private, were great; and the sight of God's work prospering in all the places was enough to have melted a heart of stone; and the thought that God, in His mercy, had made me an instrument of promoting His cause to that vast extent, has humbled me to the very dust, and made me only regret that my powers of service have not been more commensurate with my obligations to our common God and Father. My strength has continued unimpaired till this last week; but I have caught a violent cold, which has brought on the gout.

And now I will come to answer your most interesting letter. I view the sphere of India as immense, the load too heavy to be laid on any human mind, the diversities of call distracting, and the almost utter impossibility of concentrating them so as to see them all brought out into united and harmonious operation—but I had almost forgotten what an Almighty power presides, and what energies He can supply for the accomplishment of His own gracious purposes. If I forget Him, I sink; if I remember Him, not all the inconceivable load of India can overwhelm me. My comfort has been all my days, I have but *One* to please; and He is easily pleased, even in the midst of all our infirmities, when He sees only a desire to please Him. The simplicity of our work is very encouraging—in every place I see the reign of sin and Satan; and in every place I want to introduce the reign of Christ and wisdom and true holiness. Be not discouraged if you should not be able to accomplish all you wish; you have, in that respect, the portion of prophets and apostles, and of our blessed Lord Himself. You must look to the end, and see "the end of the Lord, that He is very pitiful and of tender mercy." He will prevail at last, prevail, too, by the very means which His enemies have recourse to for the counteracting of His designs. With Him at your right hand, you have none to fear; obstacles of every kind you must expect, and they will bring out to your view the secret majesty of the Most High, and enable you to realize to an inconceivable extent His unbounded power, His unerring wisdom, His incomprehensible love. I speak of these things as one who knows them by experience; I have had all the powers of earth and hell against me, but have lived to see that there are more with me than against me. That He can and does work by the meanest instruments, I am a living witness; but my sphere has been small, a mere nothing in comparison to others. Yet have I lived to see the triumph of my own principles through the land; peradventure, you also may live to see the same in your sphere. I have a perfect assurance that He who ordereth all things, both in heaven and earth, will prevail at last. Hence, then, I say, look not at minute points or difficulties, but to the Lord Himself, who will keep your mind in perfect peace, and accomplish His own pleasure through your imperfect instrumentality. . . . In truth, I love to see the creature annihilated in the apprehension, and swallowed up in God; I am then safe, happy, triumphant. And I recommend to you to enter into the chambers of all His glorious perfections, and to shut the doors about you, and there abide, till He shall have accomplished all the good purposes of His goodness both in you and by you. Nothing less than a mutual in-dwelling of God in us, and us in God, will suffice—beyond that, we want nothing. I close with imploring all imaginable blessings on your soul.

ALEXANDER KNOX.

I

VII.

Alexander Knox was born in 1758. He was private Secretary to Lord Castlereagh for some years. He lived almost entirely in Ireland, and is best known for his correspondence on religious matters. He died in 1831.

To the Rev. Dr. Alcock.

November 8, 1799.

I am sorry to tell you that whatever hopes of amendment I entertained shortly ago, are now nearly overthrown. The cold weather has attacked already my irritable nerves with such rude violence, as to make me, on the whole, as bad as ever. My case is a very distressing one. "The spirit of a man may bear his infirmity, but a wounded spirit who can bear?" How I understand these last words! Indeed, both first and last; for I have felt occasionally that a wounded spirit is a *murus aheneus* (a brazen wall).

The thing called religious melancholy may be, for aught I know, a real disease. But I do not think that it is my disease. I rather believe that religion is my master passion; and that, of course, my bad nerves work upon that, as in a covetous man they would produce apprehensions of dying a beggar.

My views of religion, when my mind is unclouded, are all cheerful and happy. I see it as a divine combination of everything that tends to exalt and to enrich human nature; and I cannot form (I hardly think I am disposed to form) any idea of comfort, even for one moment, without it. But when I think my religion is declining, that thought is my misery. Had not my disorder this power over me, it would be as harmless to me as the serpent was to St. Paul.

To the Same.

November 17, 1799.

I was sincerely concerned to hear that you have been prevented from coming to Dublin by a severe cold and rheumatism. I myself have felt so much already from the keenness of the winds, that I can easily conceive how sufficient they are to excite an insurrection in any constitution where there is either weakness in the governing powers, or disaffection in the subordinate parts. But I know also (I only wish I knew it more habitually and permanently) that disease does not, necessarily, destroy happiness.

If we are not wanting to ourselves, we may derive advantage from every situation. But there is something in indisposition (when it is not extremely painful) that has a tendency to sober the mind, to withdraw it from inferior satisfactions, and almost to force it to have recourse, not to the streams (which are so often either muddy or dry), but to the source and spring. For my own part, my ideas of real comfort are so much more associated with sickness than with health, that I am almost made uneasy by the thought of the latter. I do not wish for it, nay, I almost deprecate it. This, perhaps, is distrust in God—I fear it is; but the heart knoweth its own bitterness, and I have infinitely more bitter reflections to make on my times of health than of sickness. It is in my mind excellently arranged in our Litany, "In all time of our tribulation, in all time of our wealth;" the position of the expressions indicating a climax, and, of course, teaching in the strongest manner that prosperity is only to be feared less than death and judgment.

To George Schoales, Esq.

September 5, 1803.

Do not let your spirits droop. When they do as you describe, go into retirement, and pray solemnly and sincerely to Him that "seeth in secret," that He would make everything adverse which you meet on earth an impellent of your heart to Him—the only sure refuge and comfort. You have felt devotion, and I trust the tendency is not lessened. To acquire such a feeling where it has never yet been elicited, is, perhaps, strictly impossible with men; but to stir it up where it has been felt, is very much within human power, under that assistance which is certainly annexed to honest endeavour. Were your chagrins to be the occasion of your growing in this parent grace, you would, at length, greatly bless God for them; for invaluable is that occurrence, whatever it may be, that leads us to more habitual and deeper devotion. Judging as far as a short-sighted creature can, I should think this is the very purpose of Heaven in your present trials. You seem to me fitted to be the heir of your mother's piety. But such piety as she had, and as you have had many prelibations of, is not formed in the mind without providential helps and instruments; and as poverty of spirit is its indispensable preparative; seriousness ("blessed are they that mourn") its inseparable concomitant; and meekness its firstfruit; it seems natural, and perhaps necessary, that the outward or personal circumstances should be so disposed as to predispose to these tempers; and adverse circumstances are then surely tending to these great purposes, when they impel the mind to take refuge in God. I believe you will not disrelish this counsel; but you will be apt to think that you are too weak, too frail, and too impressible, for such a habit as that which I describe to be formed in you. To this I answer that the weakness you have to complain of is what all have, until God, in His own way, works a happy alteration, and this He really does work in as hopeless subjects, and more so than yourself. With our weaknesses, therefore, we actually have nothing to do in the way of anxiety; we have only to strive against them when they are felt, and to ask aid from God. If we so hate them in ourselves as to be cordial in our prayers for deliverance from them, God can soon and easily do that for us. A deepened sense of Himself, and of the great facts of Christianity, with a heart feeling of their spiritual intention (the crucifying us to the world, and the spiritualizing of our minds); this sentiment, I say, itself growing up within us, will bring with it the very peace and victory we look for. For the more the heart gets a concern and relish for these transcendent objects, the less its happiness is affected by the casualties of earth. "I know," says St. Paul, "both how to be abased, and how to abound." How did he learn this? Evidently thus: he had so set his mind upon, or rather his heart was so attracted and engaged by, spiritual and eternal good, that any abasement or exaltation that earthly things could cause, was to him comparatively extrinsic and trivial. While earthly things hold the affections, the feelings will rise and fall with them, and, of course, be liable to daily and hourly agitation and torment. When spiritual things are become the object of our solicitude and love, their immovableness and plenitude give us both fixedness and fulness; so that something is understood of that grand saying, "I can do all things through Christ which strengtheneth me." Certainly it requires great strength of mind to bear continued mortifications and depressions; but the humble, subdued feeling which a spiritual view of Christianity produces, and the supreme wish which it inspires to gain a complete conquest over the carnal mind, do really make these painful matters in some degree change their nature, and lose their oppressiveness. The mind gets above them, and is only concerned that it may not be "moved to do evil," a concern which God attends to and crowns with sure success.

Such are the results, I do firmly believe, of having recourse to prayer as a refuge from earthly afflictions. These happy effects are, however, not to be expected at once; but they will grow up, like the vegetation described by our blessed Saviour, "night and day, men know not how." If no pleasure is felt, no warmth perceived, that is no reason why it may not soon be felt; for such feelings spring up imperceptibly; till at length they make themselves to be felt by their reality and strength. And when this does take place, their influence is not confined to the hour; the sweet calm continues, tranquilizing the mind, rationalizing the whole conduct, and giving a new strength to bear even "the slings and arrows of outrageous fortune." I wish I felt more myself of what I have been endeavouring to describe; but I do feel enough to convince me of its blessed reality, and what I would not part with for the fee-simple of the solar system. It is truly happy to go forth into the outer walks of life, whatever those walks may be, carrying with one such a spirituality of mind as gives cheerfulness without levity, and the pleasant and prudent use of this world without the abuse. And it is yet more happy to have a predominant relish (without which the other could not be) for returning into quiet, to resume those mental, moral, and spiritual exercises and pursuits, which constitute the ultimate happiness of the soul, and which make even this desert earth a pleasant way to the heavenly country. Of this I do feel more than I once thought I ever should or could feel. So that even the severest trials which you witnessed, and still severer ones which you did not witness, are already more than compensated for in the tranquility which for the last eighteen months, but especially during the present year, has been growing up in me. Yet I am not presumptuous; for every hour makes me feel my own great weakness, and God's infinite mercy. I therefore humbly attest, in a very poor, low way, the substantial power of Christianity to give a peace which I know this world cannot give, and which I trust it cannot take away. "In the world ye shall have tribulation, but in Me ye shall have peace."

WILLIAM WILBERFORCE.

VIII.

WILLIAM WILBERFORCE was born in 1759. He took his seat in Parliament for Hull in 1780, for Yorkshire in 1784. In the same year he took up the slavery question. In 1797 he brought out his work on Christianity. He helped to organize the Church Missionary Society in 1800, and the Bible Society in 1803. The Bill for the abolition of the Slave Trade passed in 1807. He entrusted the cause of Slave Emancipation to Sir T. F. BUXTON in 1823, and retired from Parliament in 1825. He died in 1833.

THE TWO FOLLOWING LETTERS WERE WRITTEN TO HIS SISTER.

1786.

Watch and pray, read the Word of God, imploring that true wisdom which may enable you to comprehend and fix it in your heart, that it may gradually produce its effect under the operation of the Holy Spirit, in renewing the mind and purifying the conduct. This it will do more and more the longer we live under its influence; and it is to the honour of religion that those who, when they first began the Christian course, were in extremes— enthusiastical, perhaps, or rigidly severe—will often by degrees lose their several imperfections, which, though by the world laid unfairly to the account of their religion, were yet undoubtedly so many disparagements to it—like some of our Westmoreland evenings, when, though in the course of the day the skies have been obscured by clouds and vapours, yet towards its close the sun beams forth with unsullied lustre, and descends below the horizon in the full display of all his glories. Shall I pursue the metaphor, just to suggest that this is the earnest of a joyful rising, which will not be disappointed? The great thing we have to do is to be perpetually reminding ourselves that we are but strangers and pilgrims, having no abiding city, but looking for a city which hath foundations; and by the power of habit, which God has been graciously pleased to bestow upon us, our work will every day become easier, if we accustom ourselves to cast our care on Him, and labour in a true persuasion of His co-operation. The true Christian will desire to have constant communion with his Saviour. The Eastern nations had their talismans, which were to advertise them of every danger, and guard them from every mischief. Be the love of Christ our talisman.

Written on Easter Day.

April 6, 1786.

The day has been delightful. I was out before six, and made the fields my oratory, the sun shining as bright and as warm as at Midsummer. I think my own devotions became more fervent when offered in this way, amidst the general chorus with which all nature seems on such a morning to be swelling the song of praise and thanksgiving, and except the time that has been spent at church and at dinner—and neither in the sanctuary nor at table, I trust, had I a heart unwarmed with gratitude to the Giver of all good things—I have been all day basking in the sun. On any other day I should not have been so happy; a sense that I was neglecting the duties of my situation might have interrupted the course of my enjoyments, and have taken from their totality; for in such a situation as mine, every moment may be made useful to the happiness of my fellow-creatures. But the Sabbath is a season of rest, in which we may be allowed to unbend the mind, and give a complete loose to those emotions of gratitude and admiration, which a contemplation of the works and a consideration of the goodness of God cannot fail to excite in a mind of the smallest sensibility. And surely this Sabbath is, of all others, that which calls forth these feelings in a supreme degree—a frame of united love and triumph well becomes it, and holy confidence and unrestrained affection. May every Sabbath be to me, and those I love, a renewal of these feelings, of which the small tastes we have in this life should make us look forward to that eternal rest which awaits the people of God!

On the Death of his Sister, to Mrs. Wilberforce.

1816.

Our separation from each other just at this time, if it produces pain, yet reminds us of the call we have for gratitude to the Father of mercies, who has so long spared us to each other. How can I but feel this, when our dear friends' solitary situation is so forcibly impressed on me! I, indeed, have lost a most affectionate sister, one of whom I can truly say that I believe there never was on earth a more tenderly attached, generous, and faithful friend to a brother, who, though I hope not insensible to her value, saw but little of her to maintain her affection, and of whom, also, I could say much that might reasonably have abated the force and cooled the warmth of her attachment. How affecting it is to leave the person whom we have known all our lives, on whom we should have been afraid to let the wind blow too roughly—to leave her in the cold ground alone! This quite strikes my imagination always on such occasions. But there is another thing which has impressed itself in the present instance, much more powerfully than in any other I ever remember; I mean, in contemplating the face of our dear friend, to observe the fixed immovableness of the features. Perhaps it struck me more in my sister's case, because her countenance owed more of the effect it produced to the play of features than to their formation. I could not get rid of the effect produced on me by this stiff and cold fixedness for a long time. But, oh, it is the spirit, the inhabitant of the earthly tenement, not the tenement itself, which was the real object of our affection! How unspeakably valuable are the Christian doctrines and hopes in such circumstances as ours! We should not care much if we believed that the object of our tender regard had gone a few days before us, a journey we ourselves should travel; especially if we knew that the journey's end was to be a lasting abode of perfect happiness. Now, blessed be God this is after all not an illustration. It is the reality The only drawback with me here is the consciousness that I have much to do for God, and the self-reproach for not having done it. Yet here, also, I can cast myself on the sure mercies of my God and Saviour; and while I desire to do on each day the day's proper work, and to be more active and useful than I ever yet have been, still I can humbly hope that if I should be taken hence, with my work unfulfilled, He who said, "Thou didst well that it was in thy heart," will graciously forgive my sins; and that my all-merciful Saviour will take me to Himself out of the same superabundant goodness which I have ever experienced. For how true it is (I am often driven to this), Thy thoughts are not as our thoughts, nor Thy ways as our ways, for as the heavens are higher than the earth so are Thy ways higher than our ways, and Thy thoughts than our thoughts!

I think I told you that my dear sister, when asked

whether God comforted her and gave her peace, said, "Oh, yes, so much so as quite to put me to shame when I consider what a sinner I am." She then exclaimed—so like herself—"I hope this is not cant!" adding, however, "I am sure it is not all so."

To one of his Sons, on his Tenth Birthday.

I am anxious to see in you decisive marks of this great change. I come again and again, to look and see if it be indeed begun, just as a gardener walks up again and again to examine his fruit trees, and see if his peaches are set, and if they are swelling and becoming larger, finally, if they are becoming ripe and rosy. I would willingly walk barefoot from this place (near London) to Sandgate, to see a clear proof of it in my dear —— at the end of my journey.

To another Boy, aged Eleven.

My very dear Boy,

I received no little pleasure from the account Mr. L—— gave of you. I hope that, while he is absent from his earthly father, my dear —— will look up the more earnestly to that heavenly Father, who watches over all that trust in Him. Try to bring on your brother in all good, ever remembering my advice not to be satisfied with not being unkind, but trying to be positively kind. Above all, remember prayer is the great means of spiritual improvement, and guard as you would against a wild beast, which was lying in a bush by which you were to pass, ready to spring upon you—guard in like manner against wandering thoughts when you are at prayer, either by yourself or in the family. Nothing grieves the Spirit more than our willingly suffering our thoughts to wander, and fix themselves on any object which happens at the time to interest us. May God bless and keep you, my very dear boy! I think that my dear —— is greatly improved in bearing crosses of inclination properly, and I do hope that God will hear my prayers for him, and will make him a comfort and a support to my declining years. I have indulged the serious train of thought into which I ever fall in writing to my children, and am ever, my dear ——, your most affectionate father,

W. WILBERFORCE.

DANIEL WILSON.

IX.

DANIEL WILSON, Bishop of Calcutta, was born in 1778, appointed Vicar of Islington 1824, Bishop of Calcutta 1832, and died in 1857.

LETTER TO THE REV. W. JOWITT, FROM CALCUTTA.

April, 1834.

Your letter is amongst the most welcome I have received, because it is one of the most honest, and the most really simple and friendly. It does me good. I want to be reminded. I want to be stirred up. I want the comparison of minds in other latitudes. It is a strong and fatal temptation to be placed by age and circumstance of station, out of the reach of admiration and that perfect freedom of caution and advice which we all need; and then most when we think we can dispense with them.

TO ANOTHER FRIEND.

1834.

I pray you write to me from time to time. Now is the hour of temptation and trial to me. Now I have to act in circumstances of which you can have little conception—complicated, new, unexpected. I am labouring to understand my dispensation, as

Mr. Cecil would say. Two things I am sure of: to preach the gospel of my blessed Master must be right; therefore I lose no opportunity of setting forth with all boldness the name and grace of Jesus, His person, incarnation, atonement, glory, love, obedience. The other is to keep the heart—this again must be right—to keep it with all diligence, above all keeping, as that which commands the issues of life. In other matters doubt as to the particular course of duty will arise. But the mighty universal doctrine of Christ is everywhere the same, and the tender conscience, the broken heart, the watchfulness of the soul before God, are everywhere equally difficult and indispensable.

To his Brother, George Wilson.

1840.

I must write you a line to assure you of my sympathy under your long, long illness. Among those who have been brought up, my dear brother, as you and I have, in the knowledge of the truth, and who have too long resisted practical obedience to it, the grand point is the subjection of the proud, haughty will to the yoke of Christ, the deep conviction of our own sinfulness. When this is gained, all goes on rapidly. The knowledge of Christ, which before lay barren in the mind, begins to fructify. The soul casts itself on the bosom of Omnipotent mercy. The blood of atonement is sprinkled by faith on the conscience. Peace with God gradually ensues by the grace of the Holy Spirit. There is a danger, however, from a religious education not being improved, of our getting our heads full of vapid objections, idle tales, prejudices against religious persons, battlings between different doctrines of the gospel, and blasphemous suppositions about the foreknowledge and purpose of God. All these are bred in the quagmire of human pride and corruption. One grain of humility overweighs them. A broken and contrite heart falls at the feet of Almighty God, and pleads for mercy, instead of daring to speculate on infinity.

To the Same.

1841.

The impression made upon my mind by your last letter is that you are in the right way; only struggle towards the heavenly city, and you will gradually make progress, and at length obtain peace of conscience. We have received answer enough to our preceding prayers, if we are enabled to pray again. . . . Don't be in a hurry with God. If God had been in a hurry with you, where would you have been? He waited for you with all long-suffering for these thirty or forty years. *Wait now for Him.* You don't know your own heart yet; you must go deeper into its chambers of imagery. By-and-by the Lord will shine upon you. To that Lord I commend you.

To the Same.

1843.

However I may be hurried, and hurried, indeed, I am, I must write a word of love and sympathy to my beloved George, of whose sickness and weakness I have lately heard so much. Indeed, the ways of our heavenly Father are most mysterious, and to us incomprehensible; but, hereafter, we shall see the wisdom, the mercy, the necessity of every one. When your mind and spirits sink within you from pain and weakness, then resign yourself to your Father's almighty hand; if you cannot do, nor say anything, nor make any effort, float down the stream. Your gracious High Priest can be touched with the feeling of your infirmities. . . . And pray for the Holy Spirit to lift you above the dead level of this miserable world, and enable you to look beyond and over death to the bright and glorious country which lies beyond, and, as Hopeful said to Christian when passing the river of Death, "Hold up, brother, I feel the bottom," so may you rely on divine aid and grace.

To the Rev. C. Jerram.

1848.

I am most anxious to END WELL, as Bible Scott used to say. I feel nature sinking. I have not the spirits nor strength which I used to have. And my spiritual feelings sympathize with my natural. I never had much joy; I was always too conscious of the holiness of God and the obligations of the Law and Gospel, and too sensible of my own inward corruption, to be very high in joy. No, if I can creep into heaven as the poorest and vilest of sinners, I shall then be prepared to sing with an angel's voice, "Blessing, and glory, and honour, and power, to Him that sitteth on the throne, and unto the Lamb, for ever." I have a hope, but it is a faint one, in the Lord Jesus. But I am quite clear I have no other hope. I pray God that I may die with two Scripture sentences in my heart and on my lips—"God be merciful to me a sinner!" and "Lord Jesus, receive my spirit!"

To the Same.

1849.

I seem not to have heard from you for a long time. The wilderness is nearly passed to both of us, dear brother; Canaan is in view; and the Lord will be with us in passing Jordan, as He was with the Israelites. . . . On looking back on the nearly fifty years of our intimate friendship in the wilderness, what hath God wrought for us! What miracles of grace are we! How mercifully hath He borne with us! What blessings hath He showered down upon us! Farewell, my beloved friend; which of us may enter eternity first, who can tell? But God knoweth. May He be with us, and all shall be well.

To Mrs. Percival White.

1851.

You will have heard how ill I have been. I was seized with a chill, which produced internal inflammation, and at one time threatened my life. I thank God I was more calm in the prospect than I could have thought. I was enabled, and am enabled, to trust myself simply and without reserve, on the infinite atonement and propitiation of the Son of God, and on His equally boundless wisdom, love, and power. . . . Farewell, perhaps, for ever in this dying world; but in the hope of a reunion and recognition in the world above.

To a Grand-daughter, on her Confirmation.

1855.

As I hear that you have just been confirmed, I force myself to find strength and spirits to write you a word of love and counsel on the important engagement you have entered into. All depends on yourself, under God. Confirmation will of itself do you little good, unless you mean what you solemnly promised; that is, to take on you, now you are come to age, the vows made in your name at your Baptism. To this end you must pray, my love, for God's Holy Spirit to teach, to illuminate, to strengthen, and guide you. When you begin to pray from your heart, you will soon feel the reluctance of your nature. This reluctance you must overcome by God's Spirit helping you. So, when you would shut out the vanities of the world, the same opposition will arise, and must be conquered in the same way. Religion is a very gradual thing, imperceptible almost (except in the case of very extraordinary conversions), and only to be discerned, like the wind, in its effects. Therefore, go on to form good habits, and obey the voice of conscience. Consider all religious duties, not as an end, but as a means to an end. Perform all your obligations, as a scholar, a daughter, a young lady in society, with diligence and simplicity, relying on God for help, and seeking pardon for all your sins and shortcomings. Don't be discouraged because you cannot altogether do the things you aim at. You never will as long as you live. But Christ will wash you in His blood, and comfort you if you are sincere.

HENRY MARTYN.

X.

Henry Martyn was born in 1781. He entered St. John's College, Cambridge, in 1797, and took his degree as Senior Wrangler in 1801. In 1802 he made up his mind to be a Missionary, and was ordained in 1803 as Curate to Mr. Simeon. He obtained a Chaplaincy in India, and sailed in 1805. Devoted to his calling and to learning the native languages, he struggled against bad health till quite exhausted, and died at Forat, in Persia, on his way to England, in 1812.

To his Sister.

1800.

How I rejoice to find that we disagreed only about words! I did not doubt, as you suppose, at all about that joy which true believers feel. Can there be any one subject, any one source of cheerfulness and joy, to be at all compared with the heavenly serenity and comfort which such a person must find in holding communion with his God and Saviour in prayer—in addressing God as his Father, and, more than all, in the transporting hope of being preserved unto everlasting life, and of singing praises to his Redeemer when time shall be no more. Oh! I do indeed feel this state of mind at times; but at other times I feel quite humbled at finding myself so cold and hard-hearted. That reluctance to prayer, that unwillingness to come to God, who is the Fountain of all good, when reason and experience tell us that with Him only true pleasure is to be found, seem to be owing to Satanic influence. Though I think my employment in life gives me peculiar advantages, in some respects, with regard to religious knowledge; yet with regard to having a practical sense of things on the mind, it is by far the worst of any. For the labourer as he drives on his plough, and the weaver as he works at his loom, may have his thoughts entirely disengaged from his work, and may think with advantage on any religious subject; but the nature of *our* studies requires such a deep abstraction of the mind from all other things, as to render it completely incapable of anything else, and that during many hours of the day. With respect to the dealings of the Almighty with me, you have heard in general the chief of my account; as I am brought to a sense of things gradually, there is nothing peculiarly striking in it to particularize. After the death of my father, you know I was extremely low-spirited, and, like most other people, began to consider seriously, without any particular determination, that invisible world to which he was gone, and to which I must one day go. Yet, I still read the Bible unenlightened, and said a prayer or two, rather through terror of a superior power than from any other cause. Soon, however, I began to attend more diligently to the words of our Saviour in the New Testament, and to devour them with delight; when the offers of mercy and forgiveness were made so freely, I supplicated to be made partaker of the covenant of grace, with eagerness and hope; and thanks be to the ever-blessed Trinity for not leaving me without comfort. Throughout the whole, however, even when the light of divine truth was beginning to dawn on my mind, I was not under that great terror of future punishment which I now see plainly I had every reason to feel. I now look back upon that course of wickedness, which, like a gulf of destruction, yawned to swallow me up, with a trembling delight, mixed with shame at having lived so long in ignorance, error, and blindness.

To the same.

1802.

The dejection I sometimes labour under seems not to arise from doubts of my acceptance with God, though it tends to produce them; nor from desponding views of my own backwardness in the divine life, for I am more prone to self-dependence and conceit; but from the prospect of the difficulties I have to encounter in the whole of my future life. The thought that I must be unceasingly employed in the same kind of work, amongst poor ignorant people, is what my proud spirit revolts at. To be obliged to submit to a thousand uncomfortable things that must happen to me, whether as a minister or a missionary, is what the flesh cannot endure. At these times I feel neither love to God nor love to man, and in proportion as these graces of the Spirit languish, my besetting sins, pride and discontent and unwillingness for every duty, make me miserable. You will best enter into my views by considering those texts which serve to recall me to a right aspect of things. I have not that coldness in prayer you would expect, but generally find myself strengthened in faith and humility and love, after it; but the impression is so short. I am at this time enabled to give myself, body, soul, and spirit, to God, and perceive it to be my most reasonable service. How it may be when the trial comes, I know not, yet I will trust and not be afraid. In order to *do* His will cheerfully, I want love for the souls of men; to *suffer* it, I want humility. Let these be the subjects of your supplications for me. I am thankful to God that you are so free from anxiety and care; we cannot but with praise acknowledge His goodness. What does it signify whether we be rich or poor, if we are sons of God? How unconscious are they of their real greatness! and they will be so till they find themselves in glory. When we contemplate our everlasting inheritance, it seems too good to be true; yet it is no more than is due to the kindred of God manifest in the flesh. A journey I took into Norfolk last week seems greatly to have contributed to my health. The attention and admiration shown me are great and very dangerous. The praises of men do not now, indeed, flatter my vanity, as they formerly did; I rather feel pain through anticipation of the consequences; but they tend to produce, imperceptibly, a self-esteem and hardness of heart. How awful and awakening a consideration it is, that God judgeth not as man judgeth! Our character before Him is precisely as it was before or after any change of external circumstances. Men may applaud or revile, and make a man think differently of himself, but *He* judgeth of a man according to his secret walk.

To Mr. Sargent.

1803.

May you, as long as you shall give me your acquaintance, direct me to the casting down of all high imaginations. Possibly it may be a cross to you to tell me or any one of his faults. But should I be at last a castaway, or at least dishonour Christ through some sin, which for want of faithful admonition remained unmortified, how bitter would be your reflections! I conjure you, therefore, my dear friend, as you value the good of the souls to whom I am to preach, and my own eternal interests, that you tell me what you think to be, in my life, spirit, or temper, not according to the will of God my Saviour. You profess your need of humiliation. I wish my own experience could assist you in this, the most important part of our sanctification. In examining myself, according to your advice, on this head, it seems (for the work of inquiry is so exceedingly difficult that I can hardly say with certainty what I have known, or whether I have known anything on this subject) that I seek my humility rather from views of God's greatness and the example of

Christ, than of my own corruption. Now, though the former views may assist in producing the effect, yet the impressions arising from them are necessarily transient, whereas that humility which arises from just views of ourselves may be as abiding as our own consciousness, and be brought into exercise by everything we do, or speak, or think. It has greatly distressed me to think how slow my heart is to yield to the convictions of reason; how unable to mourn when it should be lying low in the dust. On reading the words of the Lord to the lukewarm Laodiceans, the form of the words is very striking and comforting, Because thou knowest not that thou art wretched, etc., I counsel thee to buy of Me eye-salve, that thou mayest see;" so that there is provision made for those whom of all others God holds most in abhorrence—the blind (to their sins), the hard-hearted, and the proud. Were it not so, what would become of me? Happily for us, the covenant is ordered in all things and sure; and it is not left to our own wisdom, but to that adorable agent, the Spirit of God, to perform that good work which He hath begun in us. May we be both conformed to the bright image of the dear Redeemer, especially in meekness and lowliness of heart!

On his way to India.

St. Salvador, November, 1805.

My mind, through the rich mercy of God, enjoys much of that peace which Christ promises to give to His people, "Peace I leave with you, My peace I give unto you." I seem to have lost a good deal of that saliency of spirits, which the company of my dearest friends, and the want of offensive objects around me, used to inspire. Here I am, and have enough to break the heart of any one who has a concern for the honour of God. I preceive it, therefore, to be my business in life not to look for enjoyment in this world, which lieth in wickedness, but to fulfil as an hireling my day, struggling against Satan, and exposed as a sheep among wolves. God has, however, so far had compassion on His unworthy servants, and the perishing souls in the ship, as to gather some of His children from among us. There is a small party of us who meet every day on the orlop-deck to sing and hear an exposition of Scripture. The rest are very hardened and contemptuous; but I trust I shall have grace to instruct in meekness those who oppose themselves. . . . Major Lambert gives me but little encouragement to hope for the conversion of the natives of India. Being strangers themselves to the power of God over their own hearts, they see only the arm of man, and therefore despair. My general reply to them is that which consoles me: "With men it is impossible, but with God all things are possible."

Serampore, July 30, 1806.

MY DEAREST LYDIA,

On a subject so intimately connected with my happiness and future ministry as that on which I am now about to address you, I wish to assure you that I am not acting with precipitancy, or without much consideration and prayer, while I at last sit down to request you to come out to me to India. May the Lord graciously direct His blind and erring servant, and not suffer the natural bias of his mind to lead him astray! You are acquainted with much of the conflict I have undergone on your account. It has been greater than you or Emma have imagined, and yet not so painful as I deserve to have found it for having suffered my affections to fasten so inordinately on an earthly object. Soon, however, after my final departure from Europe, God in great mercy gave me deliverance, and favoured me throughout the voyage with peace of mind, indifference about all worldly connections, and devotedness to no object on earth but the work of Christ. I gave you up entirely—not the smallest expectation remained in my mind of ever seeing you again till we should meet in heaven; and the thought of this separation was the less painful from the consolatory persuasion that our own Father had so ordered it for our mutual good. I continued from that time to remember you in my prayers only as a Christian sister, though one very dear to me. On my arrival in this country, I saw no reason at first for supposing that marriage was advisable for a missionary, or rather the subject did not offer itself to my mind. . . . Though I dare not say that I am under no bias, yet from every view of the subject that I have been able to take, after balancing the advantages and disadvantages that may ensue to the cause in which I am engaged, always in prayer for God's direction, my reason is fully convinced of the expediency—I had almost said the necessity—of having you with me. It is very possible that my reason may still be obscured by passion; let it suffice, however, to say that now, with a safe conscience and the enjoyment of the divine presence, I calmly and deliberately make the proposal to you; and blessed be God if it is not His will to permit it. Still, this step is not advancing beyond the limits of duty, because there is a variety of ways by which God can prevent it, without suffering any dishonour to His cause. If He shall forbid it, I think, that by His grace, I shall even then be contented, and rejoice in the pleasure of corresponding with you. . . . I can truly say, and God is my witness, that my principal desire in this affair is that you may promote the kingdom of God in my own heart, and be the means of extending it to the heathen. My own earthly comfort and happiness are not worth a moment's notice. I would not, my dearest Lydia, influence you by any artifices or false representations. I can only say that if you have a desire of being instrumental in establishing the blessed

Redeemer's kingdom among these poor people, and will condescend to do it by supporting the spirits, and animating the zeal of a weak messenger of the Lord, who is apt to grow very dispirited and languid, "Come, and the Lord be with you." It can be nothing but a sacrifice on your part to leave your valuable friends to come to one who is utterly unworthy of you, or any other of God's precious gifts; but you will have your reward, and I ask it not of you or of God for the sake of my own happiness, but only on account of the gospel. If it be not calculated to promote it, may God of His mercy withhold it! . . . Till I receive an answer to this, my prayers, you may be assured, will be constantly put up for you in this affair, that you may be under an especial guidance, and that in all your ways God may be abundantly glorified by you through Jesus Christ. You say in your letter that *frequently every day* you remember my worthless name before the throne of grace. This instance of extraordinary and undeserved kindness draws my heart towards you with a tenderness which I cannot describe. Dearest Lydia, in the sweetest and fond expectation of your being given me by God, and of the happiness which I humbly hope you might enjoy here, I find a pleasure in breathing out my assurance of ardent love. I have now long loved you most affectionately, and my attachment is more strong, more pure, more heavenly, because I see in you the image of Jesus Christ.

To the Rev. D. Brown.

Dinapore, December 3, 1806.

From a solitary walk on the banks of the river, I had just returned to my dreary rooms, and, with the reflection that just at this time of the day I could be thankful for a companion, was taking up the flute, to remind myself of your social meetings in worship, when your two packages of letters, which had arrived in my absence, were brought to me. For the contents of them, all I can say is, "Bless the Lord, O my soul! and all that is within me bless His holy name!" . . . They show me what I want to learn, that the Lord God Omnipotent reigneth—and that they that keep the faith of Jesus are those only whom God visits with His strong consolations. I want to keep in view that our God is the God of the whole earth, and that the heathen are given to His exalted Son, the uttermost parts of the earth for a possession. I have now made my calls and delivered my letters, and the result of my observations upon whom and what I have seen, is that I stand alone; not one voice is heard saying, "I wish you good luck in the name of the Lord;" not one kind thought towards me for the truth's sake.

May 4, 1807.

Your surmise about the apparent necessity of our continuing in this world in order to the diffusion of divine knowledge here, has sometimes been mine. It is useful to be reminded of our insignificancy. The Lord is not beholden to us for what we do, but in His good pleasure appoints us to this work out of numberless other instruments no less worthy, and, if we are cut off in the midst of our plans, His great scheme is not in the least degree disordered.

June 22, 1807.

What has Christianity got to contend with in this land? With the superstition and wickedness of some of its professors, and the folly and frenzy of others, what can make it triumph but divine interference? . . . I went yesterday to the native congregation, with sorrowful conviction that I was utterly unable to say anything of use unless it would please God to put it into my mouth, and prayed for a tender concern for their souls, as more desirable than the gift of speech without it, and accordingly I was helped from above, and came away refreshed in my spirit. Six soldiers came last night. To escape as much as possible the taunts of their wicked companions, they go out of their barracks in opposite directions to come to me. To encounter such scoffs spontaneously, gives one a hope of their sincerity.

To the Rev. D. Brown.

Dinapore, September 18, 1807.

I hasten to reply to your two letters. For the consolation contained in the first, I feel grateful to your kindness. The second, I am almost disposed to call the first angry letter I have received from you. However, I know it is only your love and zeal that make you grieve at my not standing forward to help your beloved church. You ascribe it to the agency of Satan. Let us hope, my dearest sir, that we shall live to see it fall out rather unto the furtherance of the gospel. I have now no choice left, as you tell me, and, therefore, it is perhaps superfluous to state again my reasons of dissent from your and Dr. B——'s opinions; yet I must write them down:—First. The evangelization of India is a more important object than preaching to the European population of Calcutta. Secondly. Therefore, he that is qualified for the first object in any degree by his youth and inclination for the work, should give himself to it, as he may hope that he has a divine call. But, thirdly. The two objects cannot be combined in such a place as Calcutta. One consequence of my joining you would be that we should get no one out from England; for they would say, Calcutta is very well supplied, Mr. Brown and Mr. Martyn are there. No, let them hear, if it must be so, that Calcutta is destitute of the gospel. Corrie and myself can always plead that we are engaged about a more important object, and then it will rest with the consciences of the ministers at home, young and old, whether they ought not to leave a small parish for the benefit of a great city. . . . My dear sir, it is our privilege to live without carefulness; especially may we be assured that the care of the Churches is with Him who has the government upon His shoulder. May He graciously direct all our ways!

Dinapore, October 24, 1807.

My dear Lydia,

Though my heart is bursting with grief and disappointment, I write not to blame you. The rectitude of all your conduct secures you from censure. Permit me calmly to reply to your letter of March 5, which I have this day received. . . . In your last letter, you do not assign among your reasons for refusal a want of regard for me. In that case I could not in decency give you any further trouble. On the contrary, you say that *present circumstances* seem to you to forbid my indulging expectations. As this leaves an opening, I presume to address you again; and till the answer arrives, must undergo another eighteen months of torturing suspense. Alas! my rebellious heart—what a tempest agitates me! I knew not that I had made so little progress in resignation to the divine will. I am in my chastisement like the bullock unaccustomed to the yoke, like a wild bull in a net, full of the fury of the Lord, the rebuke of my God. The death of my late most beloved sister almost broke my heart; but I hoped it had softened me, and made me willing to suffer. But now my heart is as though destitute of the grace of God, full of misanthropic disgust with the world, and sometimes feeling resentment against yourself and Emma and Mr. Simeon, and, in short, all whom I love and honour most; sometimes, in pride and anger, resolving to write neither to you nor to any one else again. These are the motions of sin. My love and my better reason draw me to you again. . . . I shall have to groan long, perhaps, with a heavy heart; but if I am not materially hindered by it in the work of God, it will be for the benefit of my soul. You, sister beloved in the Lord, know much of the benefit of affliction. Oh, may I have grace to follow you, though at a humble distance, in the path of patient suffering, in which you have walked so long! Day and night I cease not to pray for you, though I fear my prayers are of little value. But as an encouragement to you to pray, I cannot help transcribing a few words from my journal, written at the time you wrote your letter to me (7th March). "As on the two last days (you wrote your letter on the 5th), felt no desire for a comfortable settlement in the world, scarcely pleasure at the thought of Lydia's coming, except so far as her being sent might be for the good of my soul, and assistance in my work." How manifestly is there an omnipresent, all-seeing God, and how sure we may be that prayers for spiritual blessings are heard by our God and Father! Oh let that endearing name quell every murmur!

To the Rev. D. Corrie.

January 18, 1808.

Your conversation at the —— was curious, and, I doubt not, useful to them. The Lord endue His servants with a wisdom which all their adversaries shall never be able, etc.! If I happen to go to any place, there is a dumb silence on such subjects; they seem to be afraid to open their mouths before me; perhaps it is because I go so seldom among them that they are so shy. I now never dine out, except at the general's, once in three months. Their dinner hours are at night, and that is the time when Sabat reads his chapter in English, and we pray, and I read my Persian with him, all of which is so important to him and me, that I feel justified in what I confess my inclination inculcates—seclusion. At one family where I called this week, their unkindness amounted to incivility. On coming away, my pride told me never to enter those doors again, but charity *beareth long and is kind*, so I shall go again. You do not mention whether the pious Faqueer has been baptized yet. Whether Hindoo or Mussulman, I rejoice to bless the Lord, brother beloved, that your heart is so much toward the heathen. I am in amazement myself that —— does not stir himself to this glorious work. When I consider how much greater facilities he possesses than yourself, from long habits of study, I see that the Lord has chosen you to this honourable post. Let us pray that the Holy Spirit would endue us with great powers in the acquisition of languages; if not by supernatural gifts, yet by keeping us attentive while we read, and giving us strong and retentive memories: may He make our spirits fervent in this business! When it pleases God to open my eyes to the state of the heathen, and to the degree of good one might do, I start at my past slothfulness, and feel excited to resolve that not a moment shall be lost again. My example in this respect has a great influence upon Sabat. He is not very diligent except when he sees me so, and then he vows he will not lose a minute.

To the Same.

February 29, 1808.

After my preaching yesterday, my lassitude was so great that I could scarcely support myself. The general had not given orders for church on Saturday. I sent to inquire whether there would be service or no; in consequence of this application, an after-order was issued, to the no small disappointment of the soldiers, who were enjoying the idea of having no service. When the order came, B—— says, they vented their rage in dreadful curses and execrations against me, for they lay all the blame of having the worship of God on me. May I be always chargeable with this crime! But what sort of men are these committed to my care? Alas! they are men, of whom it is said, that their heart is at enmity with God. On the preceding Sabbath I gave them one more warning, and it is the truth grappling with their consciences that makes them thus furious. When we do meet, it is with little comfort, as you may suppose, since I know that by far the greater number come by constraint. Even Sabat, who ought to be a comforter, does by his unguarded and coarse remarks often dishearten me, for he says he does not like the public worship, and were it not that he is afraid he should be suspected of not being a Christian, he says he would not come at all. He complains that there is no love in the people, and that he is distracted and not able to pray. . . . Yet a judicious Christian would bear with all these things, and help to counteract them as much as possible. But Sabat, yet young, just thinks of pleasing himself. But through the Lord's love and mercy, I do not much need the help of man. I feel determined to combat the enemy of souls in every form. Yesterday was rather a happy day, text, "Behold, I stand at the door and knock." The poor men who continue to meet me so stedfastly in the evenings, I begin to think are really in earnest. Another came in the week, confessing his sins with tears, and desiring a hymn-book. B—— is made the butt of wicked men, who try by every species of infidel and atheistical argument within their reach to shake his faith. At the hospital,

Baxter's "Saint's Rest" seems to cut like a sharp sword. The men, when I begin, look with contempt, but presently their high looks are brought low by Baxter's plain home arguments. A few women came to my quarters yesterday. The explanation of the Lord's Prayer, from Luke xi., seemed to interest them. Saturday and to-day, two merchants have been calling on me; with each of them I discoursed a long time on the affairs of another world, telling them "not to lay up for themselves treasures on the earth." One of them said these were words of wisdom, and he would hear me further on this matter. Thus we go on, through evil report, and good report. . . . But we shall soon be out of the reach of evil, where the wicked cease from troubling. Let us continue to pray for one another, that we may be faithful unto death.

To a Friend.

Cawnpore, August 30, 1809.

I perceive from your last letter, and from what I hear of you, that we approach nearer one another in sentiment and affection. Like the sun rising to its meridian, you grow more and more warm and zealous, and my fiery zeal, if it ever deserved the name of zeal, is becoming more cool and rational. God grant that my rationality may not prove to be lukewarmness! . . . How soon critical pursuits, even when the object is the elucidation of the Word of God, lead away the heart from Him! I pray continually for divine aid in my studies; also that I may desire knowledge only to be qualified for translating and preaching the Word of God; but the language of the heart is often at variance with the words of the prayer. I beg your prayers that, after having begun in the Spirit, I may not leave off in the flesh.

Yesterday I had some very uneasy thoughts—Satan was at work in my heart; and, oh how I did envy my men at night, who were safe from the snares of increasing knowledge! In prayer with them, I could not help dwelling upon this, and found relief. Truly, love is better than knowledge. Much as I long to know what I seek after, I would rather have the smallest portion of humility and love, than the knowledge of an archangel.

To his Sister.

October, 1808.

I deserve your reproof for not having written to you oftener; and I am pained at the anxiety I have thoughtlessly occasioned you. I console myself, however, by reflecting that a letter must have reached you a few weeks after you sent your last. I am sorry that I have not good accounts to give of my health, yet no danger is to be apprehended. My services on the Lord's day always leave me a pain in my chest, and such a great degree of general relaxation, that I seldom recover it till Tuesday. A few days ago I was attacked with a fever, which, by the mercy of God, lasted only two days. I am now well, but must be more careful for the future. In this debilitating climate, the mortal frame is weak indeed; my mind seems as vigorous as ever, but my delicate frame soon calls for relaxation, and I must give it, though unwillingly; for such glorious fields for exertion open all around, that I could with pleasure be employed from morning till night. It seems a providential circumstance that the work at present assigned me is that of translation; for had I gone through the villages, as my intention led me to do, I fear that by this time I should have been in a deep decline. In my last I gave you a general idea of my employments. The society still meet every night at my quarters, and though we have lost many by death, others are raised up in their room; one officer, a lieutenant, is also given to me, and he is not only a brother beloved, but a constant companion and nurse; so you need feel no apprehension that I should be left alone in sickness; neither on any other account should you be uneasy. You know that we must meet no more in this life; therefore, since we are, I trust, both children of God by faith in Christ Jesus, it becomes a matter of less consequence when we leave the earth.

To the Rev. D. Corrie.

January 10, 1809.

Your letter from Buxar found me in much the same spiritual state as you describe yourself to be in; though your description, no doubt, belongs more properly to me. I no longer hesitate to ascribe my stupor and formality to its right cause, unwatchfulness in worldly company. I thought that any temptation arising from the society of the people of the world, at least of such as we have had, was not worthy of notice, but I find myself mistaken. The frequent occasions of being among them of late have proved a snare to my corrupt heart. Instead of returning with a more elastic spring to severe duties, as I expected, my heart wants more idleness, more dissipation. David Brainerd in the wilderness —what a contrast to Henry Martyn! But, God be thanked that a start now and then interrupts the slumber. I hope to be up and about my Master's business; to cast off the works of darkness, and to be spiritually minded, which alone is life and peace. But what a dangerous country it is that we are in! hot weather or cold, all is softness and luxury; all a conspiracy to lull us to sleep in the lap of pleasure. While we pass over this enchanted ground, call, brother, ever and anon, and ask, "Is all well?" We are as shepherds keeping watch over our flocks by night; if *we* fall asleep, what is to become of them?

To the Same.

March 3, 1809.

I did not write to you last week, because I was employed night and day on Monday and Tuesday, with Sabat, in correcting some sheets for the press.

The account of your complaint, as you may suppose, grieves me exceedingly; not because I think that I shall outlive you, but because your useful labours must be reduced to one-quarter of their present amount; and that you may perhaps be obliged to take a voyage to Europe, which involves loss of time and money. But, oh, brother beloved, what is life or death? Nothing to the believer in Jesus. "He that believeth, though he were dead, yet shall he live; and he that liveth and believeth in Me shall never die." The first and most natural effect of sickness, as I have often found, is to cloud and terrify the mind. The attention of the soul is arrested by the idea of soon appearing in a new world; and a sense of guilt is felt, before faith is exercised in a Redeemer; and for a time this will predominate, for the same faith that would overcome fear in health must be considerably strengthened to have the same ascendancy in sickness. I trust you will long live to do the work of the Lord. My discoveries * are all at an end. I am just where I was—in perfect darkness, and tired of the pursuit. It is, however, likely that I shall be constantly speculating on the subject. My thirst after knowledge is very strong; but I pray continually that the Spirit of God may hold the reins; that I may mind the work of God above all things; and consider all other things as merely occasional.

* In matters of grammar and language.

Cawnpore, April, 1810.

My dearest Lydia,

I begin my correspondence with my beloved Lydia, not without fear of its being soon to end. Shall I venture to tell you that our family complaint has again made its appearance in me, with more unpleasant symptoms than it has ever yet done? However, God, who, two years ago, redeemed my life from destruction, may again, for His Church's sake, interpose for my deliverance. Though, alas! what am I, that my place should not instantly be supplied with far more efficient instruments? The symptoms I mentioned are chiefly a pain in the chest, occasioned, I suppose, by over-exertion the last two Sundays, and incapacitating me at present from all public duty, and even from conversation. You were mistaken in supposing that my former illness originated from study. Study never makes me ill —scarcely ever fatigues me; but my lungs! death is seated there; it is speaking that kills me. May it give others life! "Death worketh in us, but life in you." Nature intended me, as I should judge from the structure of my frame, for chamber-counsel, not for a pleader at the bar. But the call of Jesus Christ bids me cry aloud, and spare not. As His minister, I am a debtor both to the Greek and the barbarian. How can I be silent, when I have both ever before me, and my debt not paid? You would suggest that energies more restrained will eventually be more efficient. I am aware of this, and mean to act upon this principle in future, if the resolution is not formed too late. But you know how apt we are to outstep the bounds of prudence when there is no kind monitor at hand to warn us of the consequences. Had I been favoured with the one I wanted, I might not now have had occasion to mourn. You smile at my allusion—at least, I hope so, for I am hardly in earnest. I have long since ceased to repine at the decree which keeps us as far asunder as the east is from the west, and yet am far from regretting that I ever knew you. The remembrance of you calls forth the exercise of delightful affections, and has kept me from many a snare. How wise and good is our God in all His dealings with His children! Had I yielded to the suggestions of flesh and blood, and remained in England, as I should have done, without the effectual working of His power, I should, without doubt, have sunk with my sisters into an early grave. Whereas, here, to say the least, I may live a few years, so as to accomplish a very important work. His keeping you from me appears also, at this season of bodily infirmity, to be occasion of thankfulness. Death, I think, would be a less welcome visitor to me, if he came to take me from a wife, and that wife were you. Now, if I die, I die unnoticed, involving none in calamity. Oh that I could trust Him for all that is to come, and love Him with that perfect love which casteth out fear! —for, to say the truth, my confidence is sometimes shaken. To appear before the Judge of quick and dead is a much more awful thought in sickness than in health. Yet I dare not doubt the all-sufficiency of Jesus Christ, nor can I, with the utmost ingenuity of unbelief, resist the reasonings of St. Paul, all whose reasons seem to be drawn up on purpose to work into the mind the persuasion that God will glorify Himself by the salvation of sinners through Jesus Christ. I wish I could more enter into the meaning of this "chosen vessel." He seems to move in a world by himself, and sometimes to utter the unspeakable words, such as my natural understanding discerneth not, and when I turn to commentators, I find that I have passed out of the spiritual to the material world, and have got amongst men like myself. But soon, as he says, we shall no longer see as in a glass, by reflected rays, but see as we are seen, and know as we are known.

To the Same.

At Sea, Coast of Malabar, February, 1811.

I sometimes try to put such a number of things together as shall produce the greatest happiness possible, and I find that even in imagination I cannot satisfy myself. I set myself to see what is that "good for the sons of men, which they should do under heaven all the days of their life," and I find that paradise is not here. Many things are delightful—some things are almost all one could wish; but yet in all beauty there is deformity; in the most perfect, something wanting; and there is no hope of its ever being otherwise, "That which is crooked cannot be made straight, and that which is wanting cannot be numbered." So that the expectation of happiness on earth seems chimerical to the last degree. In my schemes of happiness I place myself, of course, with you, blessed with great success in the ministry, and seeing all India turning to the Lord. Yet it is evident that with these joys there would be mingled many sorrows. The care of all the Churches was a burden to the mighty mind of St. Paul. As to what we should be together, I judge of it from our friends. Are they quite beyond the vexations of common life? I think not; still, I do not say that it is a question whether they gained or lost by marriage. Their affections will live when ours (I should rather say mine) are dead. Perhaps it may not be the effect of celibacy; but I certainly begin to feel a wonderful indifference to all but myself. From so seldom seeing a creature that cares for me, and never one that depends at all upon me, I begin to look round on men with reciprocal apathy. It sometimes calls itself "deadness to the world," but I much fear that it is deadness of heart. I am exempt from worldly cares myself, and therefore do not feel for others. Having got out of the stream into still water, I go round and round in my own little circle. This supposed deterioration you will ascribe to my humility, therefore I add that Mr. Brown could not help remarking the difference between what I am and what I was. . . .

February 10th.—To-day, my affections seem to have revived a little. I have been often deceived in times past, and erroneously called animal spirits, joy in the Holy Ghost. Yet I trust that I can say with truth, "To them who believe He is precious." Yes, Thou art precious to my soul, my Transport and my Trust. No thought now is so sweet as that which those words suggest, "In Christ." Our destinies thus inseparably united with those of the Son of God! What is too great to be expected? All things are yours, for ye are Christ's! We may ask what we will, and it shall be given us. Now, why do I ever lose sight of Him, or fancy myself without Him, or try to do anything without Him? Break off a branch from a tree, and how long will it be before it withers? To-day, my beloved sister, I rejoice in you before the Lord; I rejoice in you as a member of the mystic body; I pray that your prayers for one who is unworthy of your remembrance may be heard, and bring down tenfold blessings on yourself. How good is the Lord in giving me grace to rejoice with His chosen all over the earth, even with those who are at this moment going up with the voice of joy and praise, to tread His courts and sing His praise! There is not an object about me but is depressing. Yet my heart expands with delight at the presence of a gracious God, and the assurance that my separation from His people is only temporary. . . . It is sweet to reflect that we shall at last reach our home. I am here amongst men who are indeed aliens to the commonwealth of Israel, and without God in the world. I hear many of those amongst whom I live bring idle objections against religion, such as I have answered a hundred times. How insensible are men of the world to all that God is doing! How unconscious of His purposes concerning His Church! How incapable, seemingly, of comprehending the existence of it! I feel the meaning of St. Paul's words, "Hath abounded toward us in all wisdom and prudence, having made known to us the mystery of His will, that He would gather in one all things in Christ." Well, let us bless the Lord. " All Thy children shall be taught of the Lord, and great shall be the peace of Thy children."

To the Same.

Muscat, April 22, 1811.

This last marine excursion has been the pleasantest I ever made, as I have been able to pursue my studies with less interruption than when ashore. My little congregation of forty or fifty Europeans does not try my strength on Sundays; and my two companions are men who read their Bible every day. In addition to all these comforts, I have to bless God for having kept me more than usually free from the sorrowful mind. We must not always say with Watts, "The sorrows of the mind be banished from the place"; but if freedom from trouble be offered us, we may choose it rather. I do not know anything more delightful than to meet with a Christian brother, where only strangers and foreigners were expected. This pleasure I enjoyed just before leaving Bombay; a ropemaker, who had just come from England, understood from my sermon that I was one he might speak to, so he came and opened his heart, and we rejoiced together. In this ship I find another of the household of faith. In another ship which accompanies us there are two Americans who do nothing but read the Testament. . . . My kindest and most affectionate remembrances to all the Western circle. Is it because he is your brother that I love —— so much? or because he is the last come into the number? The angels love and wait upon the righteous who need no repentance; but there is joy whenever another heir of salvation is born into the family. Read Ephesians i. I cannot wish you all these spiritual blessings, since they already are all yours; but I pray that we may have the spirit of wisdom and knowledge to know that they are ours. It is a chapter I keep in mind every day in prayer. We cannot believe too much, or hope too much. Happy our eyes that they see, and our ears that they hear!

To the Same.

Shiraz, October 21, 1811.

I still continue without intelligence from India; since last January I have heard nothing from any one person that I love. My consolation is that the Lord has you all under His care, and is carrying on His work in the world by your means, and that, when I emerge, I shall find that some progress is made in India, especially the country I now regard as my own. Persia is in many respects a field ripe for the harvest. Vast numbers secretly hate and despise the superstition imposed on them, and as many as have heard the gospel approve of it, but they dare not hazard their lives for the name of the Lord Jesus. . . . Though I have complained of the inactivity of my translators, I have reason to bless the Lord that He thus supplies Gibeonites for the help of His true Israel. They are employed in a work of the importance of which they are unconscious, and are making provision for future Persian saints, whose time is, I suppose, now near. Roll back, ye crowded years, your thick array! Let the long, long period of darkness and sin at last give way to the brighter hours of light and liberty, which wait on the wings of the Sun of Righteousness! Perhaps we witness the dawn of the day of glory; and, if not, the desire we feel that Jesus may be glorified and the nations acknowledge His sway, is the earnest of the Spirit that when He shall appear we shall also appear with Him in glory.

To the Rev. C. Simeon.

1812.

I would not pain your heart, but we who are in Jesus have the privilege of viewing life and death as nearly the same, since both are ours; and I thank a gracious Lord that sickness came at a time when I was more free from apparent reasons for living. Nothing seemingly remains for me to do, but to follow the rest of my family to the tomb.

To a Friend in Cornwall.

1812.

It has pleased God to restore me to life and health again—not that I have yet recovered my former strength, but I consider myself sufficiently restored to prosecute my journey. My daily prayer is that my late chastisement may have its desired effect, and make me all the rest of my days more humble and less self-confident. Self-confidence has often let me down fearful lengths; and would, without God's gracious interference, prove my endless perdition. I seem to be made to feel this evil of my heart more than any other this time. In prayer or when I write or converse upon the subject, Christ appears to me my Life and Strength; but at other times I am thoughtless and bold, as if I had all life and strength in myself. Such neglects on our part are a diminution of our joys, but the covenant! the covenant stands fast with Him for His people evermore!

SIR THOMAS FOWELL BUXTON.

XI.

Sir Thomas Fowell Buxton was born in 1786. He entered Parliament in 1818. At Mr. Wilberforce's request, he took the lead in the movement for the abolition of slavery in 1821. The Abolition Bill was passed in 1833. Sir T. F. Buxton lost his seat in 1837. He died in 1845.

December 25, 1813.

I have often observed the advantage of having some fixed settling-time in pecuniary affairs. It gives an opportunity of ascertaining the balance of losses and gains, and of seeing where we have succeeded and where failed, and what errors or neglects have caused the failure. Now I thought, why not balance the mind in the same way—observe our progress and trace to their source our mistakes and oversights? And what better time for this than Christmas Day followed by Sunday? And what better employment of those days? So it was fixed, and consequently I refused invitation after invitation. And now for a history of my day. After breakfast, I read *attentively* the 1st of St. Peter, with some degree of that spirit with which I always wish to study the Scriptures. To me, at least, the Scriptures are nothing without prayer; and it is sometimes surprising to me what beauties they unfold, how much even of worldly wisdom they contain, and how they are stamped with the clear impression of truth, when read under any portion of this influence; and without it how unmoving they appear. . . . Well, I went to church, and I stayed for the Communion. I could not but feel grateful to see so many persons who at least had some serious thoughts of religion; especially that Charles and his wife were of the number, and, I may add, that I was also. I am not so ignorant of myself as to suppose that I have made any suitable advances. No. Every day's experience is a sufficient antidote against any such flattering delusion, for every day I see and have reason to condemn the folly, the insanity which immerses me—the whole of my mind and powers—in so trifling a portion of their interest as this world contains. But yet I feel it an inestimable blessing to have been conducted to the precincts and the threshold of truth, and to have some desires, vague and ineffectual as they are, after better things. In the evening, I sat down in a business-like manner to my mental accounts. In casting up the incidental blessings of the year, I found none to compare to my illness; it gave such a life, such a reality and nearness, to my prospects of futurity; it told me, in language so conclusive and intelligible, that here is not my abiding city. It expounded so powerfully the Scriptural doctrine of atonement, by showing what the award of my fate must be if it depended on my own merits, and what that love is which offers to avert condemnation by the merits of another; in short, my sickness has been a source of happiness to me in every way.

In 1814, after speaking of the death of John Gurney, he writes:

But it is surely from the shortness of our vision that we dwell so frequently on the loss of those who are dear to us. Are they gone to a better home? Shall we follow them? These are questions of millions and millions of centuries. The latter is but a question of a few years. When I converse with these considerations, I cannot express what I think of the stupendous folly of myself and the rest of mankind. If the case could be so transposed, that our worldly business and pleasures were to last for ever, and our religion to produce effects only for a few years, then, indeed, our, or at least my, dedication of heart to present concerns would be reasonable and prudent; then I might justify the many hours and anxious thoughts devoted to the former, and might say to the latter, "The few interrupted moments, and wandering, unfixed thoughts I spare you, are as much as your transitory nature deserves." . . . Alas! alas! how is it that as children of this world we are wiser than as children of light?

To a Boy who was very Ill.

1830.

Here I am, my dear Harry, and I will make use of my pen while tea is brewing. I have had a pleasant journey. To be sure, I could not read, for it grew dark about the time we got to Pearson's; but though I could not read out of a book, I read all the better a sermon out of the stars, and a noble sermon it was, beginning, "The heavens declare the glory of God," and ending thus, "What is man, that Thou art mindful of him?" One part of the sermon I recollect. "'Vanity, vanity, says the preacher, all is vanity.' Nay, there, Solomon, with all your wisdom, you are wrong! It may be vanity to pursue pleasure, to gratify appetite, to hunt after renown; it may be vanity to buy fine houses, acquire an estate; but it is *not* vanity, it is excellent good sense, to serve with the heart, and soul, and might, and main, the Creator of those heavens; it is not vanity to conquer evil passions, and stifle unholy repinings; it is not vanity to be patient and submissive, gentle and cheerful, during a long and weary season of trial; it is not vanity, in the midst of trials and privations, to spread around a loving and holy influence, so that the sufferer becomes the teacher and the comforter, comforting us and teaching us that unsafe we cannot be, while we are in the hands of a most merciful and tender Father!" So said the preacher to whom I was listening, and he wound up one paragraph thus, "Look at that cluster of stars, conceive the power which framed and the wisdom which guides them, and then say, if you can, 'I am able to improve on His dispensations; I can change His decrees for the better; not His will, but mine be done!'" . . . May the God of hope preserve you in all peace; help, cheer, enliven, strengthen you, and gladden you with the consolations which come from Jesus Christ!

To his Eldest Son, at Trinity College, Cambridge.

May 15, 1831.

My mind has been much turned towards you of late, and I have thought more than you might suppose of your approaching examination. Not that I am very solicitous about the result, except so far as your heart may be set on success. I should be very sorry to have you damped and disappointed, but for myself I shall be just as well satisfied with you, if you are low in the last class, as if you are high in the first. But I have a piece of advice to give you, with regard to the examination, which I am sure will, if attended to, be of service; and if you remember it and act upon it, it will be useful whenever, in your future life, you are about to engage in anything of more than usual importance. Go to God in prayer; lay before Him, as before your wisest and best friend, your care, your burden, and your wishes; consult Him, ask His advice, entreat His aid, and commit yourself to Him; but ask especially that there may be this restraint upon the efficacy of your prayers—that His will, and not your wishes, may govern the result; that what you desire may be accomplished, provided He sees it to be best, and not otherwise.

The experience of my life is, that events always go right when they are undertaken in the spirit of prayer. I have found assistance given, and obstructions removed, in a way which has convinced me that some secret power has been at work. But the assurance of this truth rests on something stronger than my own experience. "Commit thy way unto the Lord, and He shall bring it to pass;" "this poor man cried, and the Lord heard him, and saved him out of all his troubles;" "wait on the Lord, be of good courage, and He will strengthen thy heart: wait, I say, on the Lord." It is not often I give you my advice; attend to it in this instance. Depend on it, prayer is the best preparation you can have for your examination, and for everything else.

To Mrs. North, on the Death of his Friend, John Henry North.

November 20, 1831.

My dear Friend,

I have not written to you lately, partly from reluctance to intrude upon your grief, and partly from another feeling. What can I say to comfort you? There are topics of consolation for ordinary calamities; but in your case the blow has been too deep and too terrible to admit of any consolation but one, and with that I trust you are abundantly blessed. I have made known some inquiries about you, and was distressed to hear of your extreme depression; not that I wonder at it—your loss has been great indeed; but I wish to say to you, "Cheer up, my friend; the day is coming in which you will, I confidently believe, be restored to the object of your affection. The blow which has crushed your hopes and your joys with the dust, came from the hand of a most loving Father, and hereafter you will know that it was sent in mercy and loving-kindness." I heartily wish that I had sometimes the privilege of seeing you. I, too, have had very deep afflictions in my family; many of the pleasantest pictures which my imagination painted have been destroyed. This, I believe, makes my heart more susceptible of the distresses of others, and I should be glad of the opportunity of pointing out to you those passages in Scripture, and elsewhere, in which I have found comfort and relief. But if I do not see you, I do not forget you. I remember your forlorn and solitary state, and the bitter contrast between your home now and in former times. I can conceive the dreariness of it, and how constantly you must miss such a friend and companion as you have lost; but there is consolation in reflecting on what he said and what he felt in his last hours, and tracing his happy change from this sorrowful world to the inexpressible glories and joys of which he is now, I firmly trust, a partaker. This is a very painful period of the year to me. This time, almost this day, last year, I lost a son, and such a son! But God's will be done! I find that nothing so takes off the sting of my grief, as a realizing sense of his prefect happiness. My dear boy's name was *John Henry*, so named after the dearest friend of my youth.

To Mrs. Samuel Kean, on the Hopeless Illness of her Eldest Son.

September 8, 1833.

This has been but a low and gloomy day here as well as at Hampstead. I think that we have felt as sorely, and as much shared your sorrows, as if we had been on the spot. We have been in a state of much dejection since our return home, and very remarkable it has been. I had made up my mind for months that this was to be a first-rate holiday. I was to throw off my arms and my armour, and forget slavery, except now and then for a relish. In short, it was to be my business to be merry and happy at a great rate. The event has not been such. However, to-day I got rather near true comfort, and was able to ask, " Why art thou cast down, O my soul, and why art thou disquieted within me? Hope thou in God." And I do see in the event before us great stores of comfort. Nothing less than the greatest comfort would avail, for I do not disguise from myself that, all things considered (wife, father, mother, station, prospects of usefulness), it is an affliction of no common kind. Yet, dark as it is, and strongly as it proclaims that all the glory of man is as the flower of the grass, still there is that in it which tells us to gird up the loins of our mind, and rejoice and be glad. After all, in reason as well as in faith, it is no such miserable thing to be somewhat nearer than we supposed we were to that inheritance incorruptible and undefiled and glorious, which Christ has provided for His own. I hope you do not allow yourself to give way to that self-tormenting delusion of unavailing regrets and repentances, as if you had not done all you might. I think it is a narrow view to suppose that minor matters have had any weighty influence. I believe the sickness came from the hand of God. I believe from first to last it was His doing, and this consideration is sufficient to stifle all complaint as to the event, and all remorse as to the means.

In a subsequent letter to the same person, he says:

After all, we have nothing to say, in cases of human suffering and disappointment, but one thing; but that one thing carries with it supreme and all-sufficient comfort—namely, that Christ hath died for us, and hath, *actually hath*, begotten us again to a lively hope, to an inheritance incorruptible and undefiled and that fadeth not away, reserved in heaven for you and yours.

JOHN KEBLE.

XII.

JOHN KEBLE was born in 1792, at Fairford, in Gloucestershire. In 1806 he was elected Scholar of Corpus. In 1810 he took a double first degree, and in 1811 was chosen Fellow of Oriel. He was ordained deacon in 1815, priest in 1816. In 1829 he published the "Christian Year." He was elected Professor of Poetry at Oxford in 1831. He became Vicar of Hursley in 1836. In 1838 he began to be engaged in bringing out the "Library of the Fathers," and in 1846 he published the "Lyra Innocentium." In 1864 he had a paralytic seizure, and in 1866 he died.

ON THE DEATH OF HIS SISTER, MARY ANNE.

MY DEAR ———,

I knew you would be very sorry when you heard of what has come upon us, and I feel that I can write freely to you about it; but I cannot half describe to you the depth and intensity, at least so it seemed to me, of my thoughts and feelings during M. A.'s illness, and for some time since. Certainly no loss could be so great, humanly speaking, to E. and my father, but they are both such sort of people that I have long been used to consider everything that happens to them as a certain good; and there was nothing bitter in my grief as far as they were concerned, much less in thinking of

M. A. herself; but the real bitterness was when I thought of many things in which I have been far less kind to her than I ought to have been. Somehow or other, I have for years been accustomed to talk to her far more freely than to anybody else in the world, though of course there were two or three whom I loved quite as well; but it has so happened that whenever I was moody or fretful, she has had to bear with me more than any one; and if I choose I could sit down and torment myself by the hour with the thought of it. This is the only feeling of real bitterness that I have on the subject, but I know it is wrong to indulge it, and I trust soon to get over it entirely; indeed, I seem to have done so already, only I feel one cannot in any way depend upon one's self. I am certain no person who believes in the atonement ought to indulge in bitter remorse, and, therefore, by God's blessing, I don't mean to be uncomfortable if I can help it, even in the thought of my past faults. I have been so too much already, and it only serves to make one lazy, and weaken one's own hands and one's friends'. If you please, therefore, don't let us encourage one another in melancholy any more, but let us always resolutely look to the bright side of things; and, among other helps to be quiet, let us always talk as freely to one another as we do now, for nothing relieves one so much as making a clean breast.

I never was so much impressed with the value and excellency of cheerfulness as a Christian virtue, as I have been since M. A.'s death. The remembrance of her peculiar cheerfulness (for she had more of it than any of us, except, perhaps, my father) goes so far towards keeping us all up, especially E. We keep thinking how vexed she would be to see us annoying ourselves about her, and how she always wanted everybody to live in sunshine, and it quite makes us ashamed and afraid to feel desolate. You may easily imagine what a support this is to E., whose thoughts, both from her temper and circumstances, are more entirely fixed on M. A. than either of ours can be. Of course, she must feel like a widow, but I trust not as a desolate one; certainly she seems alive to every comfort, and her prevalent feeling is one of deep thankfulness for the assurance of M. A.'s happiness. . . . I like your plans of reading; but don't be disheartened if you seem to do little; only I would not indulge in reveries. As you speak of good books, do look at the life of Mr. Donnell, if it comes in your way. It is in the list of the Christian Knowledge Society. See p. 153; there is a passage which I have often found useful, and I suspect you may too. You cannot think how often you come to my mind, especially now I am endeavouring to train myself to a more thorough content and cheerfulness than I have ever yet practised. For I fancy that you and I require in some respects the same sort of training. At any rate, I know too well what passes in my own mind, to think anything contemptible in you. Now I think this is enough about ourselves, for I hold it to be a selfish and dangerous sort of thing for people to be always turning their eyes inward. But don't let this hinder you from writing always as freely of whatever is uppermost as you do now; only please not to let your own faults, or anything uncomfortable, be often uppermost. As I said before, I am sure it is not natural it should be so in those for whom Christ died. This lesson I have learnt of dear M. A., and I hope not to forget it, but to have it perfect by the time I see her again; and if I can get you to have it too, so much the better for us all. She often used to speak of you, and I dare say to pray for you, for she fancied you not quite comfortable, and she had a great feeling for that sort of discomfort. God bless you now, my dear friend. Let me hear from you as often as it seems to do you any good, and don't mind what you write.

To a Friend, on the Death of his Infant Child.

It is presumptuous in me, I know, to pretend to comfort you on so sad an occasion as this, but I *must* tell you truly that my heart bleeds at the thought of your loss, though I know it is absolutely impossible for me to sympathize with you under it; but you have better comforters who do, not only —— and dear ——, but a more effectual one than either, even Him, who, when He saw a dead man carried out, the only son of his mother, had compassion on her. He is even now touched with a feeling of the sorrow of heart which has fallen upon you and your dear wife, whom God bless, confirm, and comfort, for His sake.

My dear friends, think as little as you can of yourselves, but think of the blessed infant whom you presented so few days ago before Christ, in His earthly temple; think of her being even now admitted to serve Him in His heavenly temple, day and night, and knowing and praising Him infinitely better than the greatest saint on earth can do. And though it is nothing in comparison of Eternity, yet it is blessing enough to assuage your grief—which, however good and Christian, must confess itself to be but earthly—when you consider that your darling is put into her Saviour's arms so many years before the time that most of His servants are admitted there, *quite* safe, *quite* good, *quite* happy, and, I dare to say it, overflowing with love for you, beyond what all your kindness and tenderness could have made her comprehend in the longest life that parents and children can expect to enjoy together here. And although David said that his child could not return to him, yet, since we are taught that there is a sympathy between paradise and earth, at least between the saints in one and the saints in the other; what if Christian parents, by holy living, should be supposed to have this comfort among others, that their lost children still watch over them, or in some way or another know of their well-doing? The thought is not, I am persuaded, unscriptural, but, thank God, you have no need of it. "For if we believe that Jesus died and rose again, even so them also which sleep in Jesus will God bring with Him." You need not look further for comfort than these words. May He in whom alone we can know comfort, make them and all other consolations which His providence has in store for you so truly comfortable to you, that you shall be able to look backward, even to this sad time, with humble thankfulness to Him for helping you to suffer as Christians!

To a College Friend, on Changing his Profession.

1819.

We are not, God be thanked, in our own hands, but in the hands of One who loves us infinitely better than we do ourselves. If we could but once possess ourselves with that belief (which yet is more certain than anything which we do not see with our eyes), how little, comparatively, would such trials as these appear to us—in comparison, I mean, with the least sin! And yet we commit great sins every day, as if they were things of course. Indeed, we all need one another's prayers very much, but not always in those respects most in which our friends are apt to suppose we need them most. How comfortable to think that there is one Friend from whom none of our necessities can be hid, and who cares for them all, if we have not wilfully rejected His care!

I am sure I need not apologize for writing in this

strain to you, who are so possessed, as I trust, with the love of our dear Master, that you would be glad to dedicate yourself entirely to His more special service and ministry. But persevere with a good heart, my dear fellow, where you are, and do not doubt that Providence will give you opportunities enough of being useful. And, perhaps, to any man who would fain be in the clerical profession, but is hindered by circumstances, it may not be amiss to consider that, if the chance of doing good is increased, the responsibility is increased along with it, and it is a fearful thing to think that one owes a heavier debt than one's fellows to the Great Owner of all—aye, so fearful, that nothing would enable one to support the thought, except it were the same recollection with which I ended the last paragraph, and with which, if we brought it in as often as we have occasion, we should end every paragraph and every sentence which we write or speak, *i.e.*, that we have One who has redeemed our infinite debt, as well as promised us unfailing supplies for the future.

To a Friend, on the Strictness of our Lord's Teaching in the Gospel.

1823.

You see already what an unworthy choice of an adviser you have made, by my long delay in answering your very kind letter, which affected me a good deal in various ways, and not least with shame at finding myself, as without foolish affectation I really did, so utterly unprepared and unworthy to be so trusted. I thought I would give myself a little time to think over the points mentioned in your letter. But in so scrambling and dissipated a way does one proceed, that I fear I have not thought to any good purpose of the first; . . . as to the second, all the time I can spare . . . has long been devoted to thinking of it. And as it is so much the more important of the two, . . . I will speak to it first.

The plain truth then is, my dear friend, that I have no doubt whatever that the misgivings you feel about the great strictness of the gospel precepts —of our Saviour's advice, more particularly—are perfectly right and reasonable; and the more you allow them, in a quiet way, to influence you in practice, the happier and wiser you will be. It is nothing in the world, I am almost certain, but the degeneracy of the Christian Church (foretold in the Scriptures as plainly as possible) which makes people turn away from certain precepts as if they were too strict to be practised, and have recourse to so many poor miserable shifts to get rid of them. And I think, as a general rule, one of the best remedies for this would be to consider these commandments as so many instances of *friendly advice*, rather than as so many tasks set us; not to deal with them as conditions, arbitrarily appointed, before one shall be allowed to enter into heaven, but as practices and tempers of mind, naturally and reasonably flowing from what we know to be the truth of our condition and of God's dealings with us. For instance, when the question is about such a precept as St. Matt. xix. 21, we are not to be nicely inquiring how much money is to be given in alms, but we are to consider whether it is not natural and reasonable for one who sincerely believes the gospel, to lay out every farthing in some way which deserves to be called alms, *i.e.*, in providing for the reasonable wants of others rather than his own superfluities, however innocent in themselves these may be. It is much better, as far as I can judge, on many accounts, to ask ourselves rather what is reasonable? than what is necessary? The same may be said of humility, forgiveness of injuries, self-denial, devotional exercises, and, indeed, every part of the Christian life. Now, if one looks at things in this light, judging always of what is reasonable and natural with a view to the next world, I allow it will be quite impossible not to feel sorrow and shame and fear very often, perhaps oftener than not, both for one's self, and for those committed to one's charge. But still this is perfectly consistent with a "cheerful view of religion"; indeed, the more cheerfully one looks at that, the higher hopes one entertains, and the more one's heart is set upon the glorious destinies in store for us, the more painful must be the thought how sadly we have abused, and too often are abusing and neglecting, such talents. Who so cheerful in religion as St. Paul? Yet he honestly owned himself the chief of sinners in his own eyes. Depend upon it, if a man does but try to *act up* to these views, especially in the matter of humility; and if he always goes upon what is reasonable and not upon mere feeling—indeed, not at all by feeling, if he can help it—he will not want cheerfulness in his religion, neither will he despond, however ill he may think of things. He will be as much awake as a bold and skilful seaman in a storm, who knows how much his own safety and that of his messmates depends on his keeping up his spirits, and doing his best.

To a Clergyman, on Amusements.

1860.

Your communication is most deeply interesting. I only wish I may be able to speak truth and comfort for such a person as you describe. I feel very stupid; one can but try. All my life long I have been used to take what many would call the *laxer* view of common recreations and the ordinary pleasures of life, supposing them, of course, innocent in themselves, and not so indulged in as to give scandal, or withdraw the heart from God; and leaving it free to those who feel themselves inwardly called, and providentially encouraged, to something higher—something like counsels of perfection—to take their course.

The whole tenor of Holy Scripture, as expounded by the Church in all ages, and not least clearly by our own standard teachers, appears to me to bear out this view. Only think what a treasure of *secondary satisfactions* (so to call them) the Bible itself is; the perfection of poetry, language, and history; its blessings on conjugal love, family delights, the ways of little children, the beauties and mysteries of art and nature! It seems to say, "Take all these, and make much of them, for God's glory; be assured that there is nothing so innocent or trifling that it may not be thus sacrificed to Him." And when our Lord says, "Woe to them that laugh," etc., I understand Him to be warning us against a frivolous worldly temper, not against the moderate indulgence of the instinct which prompts laughter, to cheer those who need cheering, or sometimes, in a warning way, to correct those who need correcting. In all this, I believe, I concur with such writers as Hooker, Bishop Taylor, George Herbert, Isaac Walton, etc., not to mention foreign writers. I should think the best and most blessed way for young persons . . . . would be to go upon these principles, watching themselves very carefully. . . . I would point out that even in the life which is most secular there is room for the greatest Christianity in all parts of life.

To a Lady, on Spiritual Dryness.

I have just been reading over your letter, and am more vexed than I can say, though not half so vexed as I ought to be with myself, for not having answered it. . . . And now, what can I say more than you have heard and read in a much better form many times before? One thing I *will* say, for I am most firmly persuaded of it, that a great part of your dullness and dryness about holy things, probably the whole, so far as it is accountable for by the human judgment, is a symptom of your illness; and I dare say you often feel the like distressing want of interest in other matters which you would fain take interest in. I dare say you often have to rouse yourself up, and force yourself to be or seem amused with things which in former days would have taken hold of you without any effort. If it is so in ordinary things, then its not being so in religious services and meditations would be a merciful interference, more, perhaps, than one could reasonably expect, and its not being granted ought not to dishearten one, nor make one think one's self the subject of a special judgment. Another thing is that all religious meditation has a tendency, if it be not its direct work, to turn the mind's eye back as it were on itself; and this is necessarily a painful and wearisome effort, and causes a sort of aching, which cannot be well endured, when the frame or spirits are weakened by sickness of certain sorts. I suppose, then, that it is a provision of God's mercy to disqualify the mind in such cases for meditation, and keep it in a kind of dullness, which, however uncomfortable, may be as good for the soul and mind as sleepiness (which is often also most uncomfortable) is for the body. Anyhow, it is, and must be, a grief to you, and so far part of His Fatherly discipline; but if conscience, fairly examined, charges you with no more than you have by His grace truly confessed and repented of (though that were *ever* such deadly sin), you must not take this, any more than other troubles, as a token of wrath, but as an earnest (how strange soever it may seem to us) of great love hereafter to be revealed—pardoning love, inexhaustible, everlasting love. O, my dear child, only think of the joy and consolation, when all that is now crooked shall be made straight, and all that is wanting shall be numbered, and His forgiven ones shall see, once for all, how these distresses have served to purge them, perhaps, and make them white, and otherwise prepare them to see His face with joy!

In the mean time, I beg of you, do not be too severe, do not strain your inward eye by turning too violently back upon itself; remember, you are bound for others' sake, as well as your own, to be if you can, and not only to seem, comfortable and cheerful. Do not be afraid to take, as they come, the refreshments and amusements which His mercy provides for you, and be not too nice in comparing your interest in these with the dullness you may possibly feel in direct religious exercises. Take a lesson from your little ones (may He be with them!) and be patient, or cheerfully thankful, as the case may be, without blaming yourself for what is in all probability God's visitation, no direct fault of your own.

On Speaking Freely of the Departed.

I need not say to you, because you must know it full well, how desirable it is to lose no time in using ourselves to speak freely and calmly to one another of those who are out of sight, as though they were, as they are, *only* out of sight.

To a Lady, an Entire Stranger, on Repentance.

I am very anxious that you should be quite aware of one thing . . . . that the wish, the *continued wish*, to be contrite, *is* contrition; the *wish* to hate one's evil self is the beginning of such hatred. A person who feels it in the slightest degree, and encourages the feeling, and tries to have more of it, and is grieved not to have more; such a one so far is surely coming to our Lord, and him that is coming unto Him, He will in no wise cast out. Undoubtedly the first effort at all this will be very faint and imperfect, but so are all our beginnings, and our perceiving them to be such is a good sign, and not a bad one. The only sure and sufficient test of reality in one's feelings, I suppose to be our *conduct, i.e.,* our deliberate thoughts, our words, and our actions, and especially in little, everyday, unnoticed and unnoticeable matters; if we are gradually trying more and more to bring them into captivity to the love of God and our neighbour, we may have the comfortable hope that God accepts our repentance, however imperfect. In your own case, if I understand your letter rightly, submission to a great degree of spiritual loneliness seems a main part of the trial. If you can submit to doubt, perplexity, misgivings, even to desolation, as to bereavement or bodily pain, striving to make the best of it, and take it cheerfully as part of His gracious dealings with you, and putting down every complaining thought, either of your personal or ecclesiastical position, I trust that in His good time you will find that you are in a sure and safe way.

To a Young Layman: Hints on Self-Guidance.

It is so rare in our profession to find one's self treated with real confidence, especially by young persons, that when such a thing does happen, one feels quite refreshed by it. For my sake, therefore, as well as your own, let me beg of you to address me, and tell me things without scruple, as long as I can be of any use to you, or to any one for whom you are interested. I do not wonder at the feeling you express to me of dread as to what may happen by-and-by, when your situation is a more dangerous one, nor at your almost seeming a hypocrite in your correspondence with me. We are, almost all of us, such double-minded persons, our best moments so miserably unlike our worst, that it is but natural we should sometimes feel so, and then our enemy will endeavour to make us think it is all over with us, at least for the present, and that we may just as well be consistent, at least for a time, in pursuit of present enjoyment; but let me beg of you not to listen to him, but rather to the good angels, who would make you consistent the other way. Perhaps, left as you are to yourself, it may help you towards this happy result if you keep, at least for a time, some sort of register of your advances or relapses in those matters on which your conscience most troubles you—something very brief, only just sufficient to help the memory, and if it were in shorthand, or in some kind of cipher, so that, even if mislaid, it might betray nothing—this would lessen one objection to the practice. . . . In the mean time, be of good heart, and never permit your mind to indulge in any kind of despondency. Our Lord's rule, "Take no thought for the morrow," may well be applied to this matter, as well as to others merely temporal.

To a Lady, on the Absence of Conscious Love and Devotion.

I am truly sorry for your distress; yet in substance I fear I can say little to help you that I have not said before. It is a trouble to be borne, this consciousness of being so dull and dry when you least wish to be so; only take care that you do not grow impatient, as though you were hardly used in its being allowed; neither be too minute in searching out the reason of it, only let it make you more watchful of your general conduct, especially against the infirmities of your temper. Take care that you do not ask angrily, "Must I continue to serve God in slavish fear?" Of course you must, if it be His will. Is it not infinitely better than not serving Him at all? Do not dwell upon this subject. Do not allow yourself to be worked up into any bitter feelings about it. Every morning, as earnestly as you can, commit yourself in prayer concerning it to our loving Saviour, and then dismiss it. Do not fret about it between whiles; you cannot help being grieved at it when it occurs in private or public devotion, but then also dismiss it as well as you can at the end, by an earnest wish before God, which wish will be in His ears a prayer, that He would forgive you what in it may be due to any fault of your own, and enable you to mend it; and for the rest that He would either relieve it, or enable you to bear it as He knows to be best for you; and especially pray against bitterness.

To a Father, on the Death of his Son.

What can I say to you .... to thank you as I know I ought for your most comfortable letter? I knew it would be full of comfort, but this somehow is beyond my expectation; ... it looks to me like a fresh world opened for you, both of sorrow and of consolation. Well do I know what thoughts I ought to have of it, so far as I am myself concerned; but for you all, one's heart can rest in nothing but leaving you, as it were, to Him whom you can all but see taking your child up in His arms, and giving him His final blessing. I hope not to forget what you speak of in my prayers, such as they are; I shall ask that for which I hope as confidently as I well can for any special mercy, that this merciful trial may be fully blessed to all the purposes for which it is sent—for correction where need may be; for high and heavenly improvement to you all. May you have many a more joyful Christmas! I do not think you will ever have a much *happier* one in this world. Forgive me if I say what I ought not. Your letter this morning met one from ——, with a similar account of his only boy. . . . This evening brings a much worse account than any before of ——. So His people seem to be fast entering into their rest, or rather, His rest.

THOMAS ARNOLD

XIII.

THOMAS ARNOLD was born in 1795. In 1814 he took a first-class degree at Oxford, and in 1815 was elected Fellow of Oriel. In 1827 he was elected Head-master of Rugby. In 1841 he became Regius Professor of Modern History at Oxford, and in June, 1842, he died suddenly at Rugby.

TO A PUPIL, WHO HAD WRITTEN WITH MUCH ANXIETY, TO KNOW WHETHER HE HAD OFFENDED HIM, AS HE THOUGHT HIS MANNER CHANGED TOWARDS HIM.

July, 1833.

The other part of your letter at once gratified and pained me. I was not aware of anything in my manner to you that could imply disapprobation; and certainly it was not intended to do so. Yet it is true that I had observed, with some pain, what seemed to me indications of a want of enthusiasm, in the good sense of the word, of a moral sense and feeling corresponding to what I knew was your intellectual activity. I did not observe anything amounting to a sneering spirit; but there seemed to me a coldness in religious matters, which made me fear lest it should change to sneering as your understanding became more vigorous; for this is the natural fault of the undue predominance of the mere intellect, unaccompanied by a corresponding growth and liveliness of the moral affections, particularly that of admiration and love of moral excellence; just as superstition arises, where it is honest, from the undue predominance of the affections, without the strenghening power of the intellect advancing in proportion. This was the whole amount of my feeling with respect to you, and which has nothing to do with your conduct in school matters. I should have taken an opportunity of speaking to you about the state of your mind, had you not led me now to mention it. Possibly my impression may be wrong, and indeed it has been created by very trifling circumstances; but I am always keenly alive, on this point, to the slightest indications, because it is the besetting danger of an active mind—a much more serious one, I think, than the temptation to mere personal vanity. I must again say, most expressly, that I observed nothing more than an apparent want of lively moral susceptibility. Your answers on religious subjects were always serious and sensible, and seemed to me quite sincere; I only feared that they proceeded, perhaps too exclusively, from an intellectual perception of truth, without a sufficient love and admiration for goodness. I hold the lines "Nil admirari," etc., to be as utterly false as any moral sentiment ever uttered. Intense admiration is necessary to our highest perfection, and we have an object in the gospel, for which it may be felt to the utmost, without any fear, lest the most critical intellect should tax us justly with unworthy idolatry. But I am as little inclined as any one to make an idol out of any human virtue or human wisdom.

To a Person who had once been his Landlord, and was ill of a Painful Disorder, but refused to see the Clergyman of his Parish, or allow his Friends to address him on Religious Subjects.

I was very sorry to see you in such a state of suffering, and to hear from your friends that you were so generally. I do not know that I have any title to write to you; but you once let me speak to you when I was your tenant about a subject on which I took it very kind that you heard me patiently, and, trusting to that, I am venturing to write to you again. I have myself been blessed with very constant health; yet I have been led to think from time to time, what would be my greatest support and comfort, if it should please God to visit me, either with a very painful or a very dangerous illness; and I have always thought, that in both, nothing would do me so much good, as to read, over and over again, the account of the sufferings and death of Christ, as given in the different Gospels. For, if it be a painful complaint, we shall find that in mere pain He suffered most severely, and in a great variety of ways; and if it be a dangerous complaint, then we shall see that Christ suffered very severely from the fear of death, and was very sorely troubled in His mind, up to the very time almost of His actual dying. And one great reason why He bore all this, was that we might be supported and comforted when we have to bear the same. But when I have thought how this would comfort me, it is very true that one cannot help thinking of the great difference between Christ and one's self; that He was so good, and we so full of faults and bad passions of one kind or another. So that if He feared death, we must have much greater reason to fear it; and so, indeed, we have, were it not for Him. But He bore all His sufferings that God might receive us after our death, as surely as He received Christ Himself. And surely it is a comfort above all comfort, that we are not only not suffering more than Christ suffered, but that we shall be happy after our sufferings are over, as truly as He is happy. Dear Mr. ———, there is nothing in the world which hinders you and me from having this comfort but the badness of our hearts, which will not let us open ourselves heartily to God's love towards us. He desires to love us, and to keep us, but we shut ourselves up from Him, and keep ourselves in fear and misery, because we will not receive His goodness. Oh how heartily we should pray for one another, and for ourselves, that God would teach us to love Him, and be thankful to Him, as He loves us! We cannot, indeed, love God if we keep any evil or angry passion within us. If we do not forgive all who may have wronged or affronted us, God has declared most solemnly that He will not forgive us.

There is no concealing this, or getting away from it. If we cannot forgive, we cannot be forgiven. But when I think of God's willingness to forgive me every day, though every day I offend Him many times over, it makes me more disposed than anything else in the world to forgive those who have offended me; and this, I think, is natural, unless our hearts are more hard than with all our faults they commonly are. If you think me taking a liberty in writing, I can only beg you to remember that, as I hope Christ will save me, so He bids me try to bring my neighbours to Him also; and especially those whom I have known, and from whom I have received kindness. May Christ save us both, and turn our hearts to love Him and our neighbours, even as He has loved us and has died for us!

To J. C. PLATT, ESQ.

February 4, 1837.

To read an account of Christ written as by an indifferent person, is to read an unchristian account of Him; because no one who acknowledges Him can be indifferent to Him, but stands in such relations to Him, that the highest reverence must ever be predominant in his mind when thinking or writing of Him. And again, what is the impartiality required? Is it that a man shall neither be a Christian, nor yet not a Christian? The fact is, that religious veneration is inconsistent with what is called impartiality, which means that as you see some good and some evil on both sides, you identify yourself with neither, and are able to judge of both. And this holds good with all human parties and characters, but not with what is divine, and consequently perfect; for then we should identify ourselves with it, and are perfectly incapable of passing judgment upon it. If I think that Christ was no more than Socrates (I do not mean in degree, but in kind), I can, of course, speak of Him impartially—that is, I assume at once that there are faults and imperfections in His character, and on these I pass my judgment; but if I believe in Him, I am not His judge, but His servant and creature, and He claims the devotion of my whole nature, because He is identical with goodness, wisdom, and holiness. Nor can I, for the sake of strangers, assume another feeling and another language, because this is compromising the highest duty—it is like denying Him, instead of confessing Him. This all passed through my mind when I heard that the article was written in a purely historical tone, and yet stated the resurrection as a matter of fact. Now, if the resurrection be true, Christianity surely is true; and then how can any one think of Christ except religiously?

To an Old Pupil.

April 5, 1837.

I take this opportunity to answer your kind and interesting letter, for which I beg you to accept my best thanks. I can hardly answer it as I could wish, but I do not like to delay writing to you any longer. Your account of yourself and of that unhealthy state of body and mind under which you have been labouring, was very touching to me. I rejoice that you were recovering from it, but still you must not be surprised if God should be pleased to continue your trials for some time longer. It is to me a matter of the deepest thankfulness that the fears which I had at one time expressed to you about yourself have been so entirely groundless; we have the comfort of thinking that with the heart once turned to God, and going on in His faith and fear, nothing can go very wrong with us, although we may have much to suffer and many trials to undergo. I rejoice, too, that your mind seems to be in a healthier state about the prosecution of your studies. . . . I trust that you will gain a good foundation of wisdom in Oxford, which may minister in after years to God's glory and the good of souls; and I call by the name of wisdom—knowledge, rich and varied, digested and combined, and pervaded through and through by the light of the Spirit of God. Remember the words, "Every scribe instructed to the kingdom of God, is like unto a householder who bringeth out of his treasure *things new and old;*" that is, who does not think that either the first four centuries on the one hand, nor the nineteenth on the other, have a monopoly of truth, but who combines a knowledge of one with that of the other, and judges all according to the judgment which he has gained from the teaching of the Scriptures. I am obliged to write more shortly than I could wish; let me hear from you when you can, and see you when you can, and be sure that, whether my judgments be right or wrong, you have no friend who more earnestly would wish to assist you in that only narrow road to life eternal, which I feel sure that you, by God's grace, are now treading.

To J. L. Hoskyns, Esq., in Answer to a Question on the Preface to the Third Volume of Sermons.

September 22, 1839.

It is the peculiar excellence of the Christian ministry, that there a man's professional reading and general reading coincide, and the very studies which most would tend to make him a good and a wise man, do, therefore, of necessity, tend to make him a good clergyman. . . . That the knowledge of the Scriptures is the most essential point in our studies as men and Christians, is as clear to my mind as that it is also the most essential point in our studies as clergymen. The only question is, in what manner is this knowledge to be best obtained. Now —omitting to speak of the moral and spiritual means of obtaining it, such as prayer and a watchful life, about the paramount necessity of which there is no doubt whatever—our present question only regards the intellectual means of obtaining it, that is, the knowledge and cultivation of our mental faculties which may best serve to the end desired. Knowledge of the Scripture seems to consist of two things, so essentially united, however, that I scarcely like to separate them, even in thought: the one I will call the knowledge of the contents of the Scriptures themselves; the other the knowledge of their application to us, and our own times and circumstances. ... And it is this second part which requires such a variety of miscellaneous knowledge, inasmuch as in order to apply a rule properly we must understand the nature and the circumstances of the case to which it is to be applied, and how they differ from those of the case to which it was applied originally. Thus there are two states of the human race which we want to understand thoroughly—the state when the New Testament was written, and our own state. And our own state is so connected with, and dependent on, the past, that in order to understand it thoroughly we must go backwards into past ages, and thus, in fact, we are obliged to go back till we connect our time with the first century, and in many points with centuries yet more remote. You will say, then, in another sense from what St. Paul said it, "Who is sufficient for these things?" and I answer, "No man;" but notwithstanding, it is well to have a good model before us, although our imitation will fall short of it. But you say, "How does all this *edify?*" And this is a matter which I think it is very desirable to understand clearly. If death were immediately before us—say that the cholera was in a man's parish, and numbers dying daily—it is manifest that our duties, our preparation for another life, by conforming ourselves to God's will respecting us in this life, would become exceedingly simple. To preach the gospel, that is, to lead men's faith to Christ as their Saviour by His death and resurrection; to be earnest in practical kindness; to clear one's heart of all enmities and evil passions; this would be a man's work and this only; his reading would, I suppose, then be limited to such parts of the Scriptures as were directly strengthening to his faith and hope and charity; to works of prayers and hymns; and to such practical instructions as might be within his reach as to the treatment of the prevailing disease. Now, can we say that in ordinary life our duties can be made thus simple? Are there not, then, matters of this life which must be attended to? Are there not many questions which would press upon us besides the simple, direct preparation for death? And it being God's will that we should have to act and advise in these things, and our service to Him and to His Church necessarily requiring them—is it right to say that the knowledge which shall teach us how to act and advise rightly with respect to them is not *edifying?* . . . A man may do immense good with nothing more than an unlearned familiarity with the Scriptures, with sound practical sense and activity, taking part in all the business of the parish, and devoting himself to intercourse with men rather than with books. I honour such men in the highest degree, and think that they are among the most valuable ministers that the Church possesses. A man's reading in this case is of a miscellaneous character, consisting, besides the Bible and such books as are properly devotional, of such books as chance throws in his way, or the particular concerns of his parish may lead him to take an interest in. And though he may not be a learned man, he may be that which is far better than mere learning—a wise man and a good man.

MARIA HARE.

XIV.

MARIA LEYCESTER was born in 1798. In June, 1829, she married AUGUSTUS HARE. He had just been appointed Rector of Alton Barnes, in Wiltshire, where they lived until bad health compelled him to go abroad. He died in February, 1834. Mrs. HARE lived till November, 1870. The letters are taken from "Memorials of a Quiet Life."

To L. A. S.

July 10, 1827.

What a pleasure it is to think that the most exquisite moments on earth are but faint images of that which will be! In beautiful days and nights, such as these, how far easier is it to raise one's thoughts, and lift one's self up to higher spheres, and what a miserable and aching void must those hearts feel which cannot ascend beyond the present! When we look around at a world so beautiful, our hearts must glow with gratitude for having so much of enjoyment given; and if there are some things which are kept from us; if we have some trials, some annoyances; if all is not as we could wish it; we must see the mercy of it in leading us to seek that comfort which, if every earthly blessing were granted to us, we might perhaps neglect and forget. Oh, at times, how clear, how straight, seems the path we should follow, making one object our great and chief concern, and all things subservient to that; forgetting ourselves except in the exercise of examining self, and striving to show worthily our Christian profession by a more unwearied endeavour after good, and love to all around us! But then comes human weakness, and our highest resolves often fall, and become of no avail; this, too, has its use, for without such humbling experience we should not fly to Him who alone can make us strong. We shall never be tried beyond what we are able to bear, and assuredly those whose struggle here has been the strongest, will hereafter reap the more abundantly. I close every evening now by learning a hymn of my dear Reginald's, which sends me to sleep in peace and love. You are hardly aware in reading them how calculated they are for private devotion.

To the Same.

July 29, 1827.

Augustus is just gone. . . . It is indeed a blessed thing in a world which it needs not eight and twenty years to show in its true colours, to feel the repose of resting upon the certain hope of devoted affection, and a peaceful and happy future; and although for *his* sake I could wish for more lightness and gaiety of heart than ever comes to me now, I am quite satisfied for my own that the past has not been in vain, and that it is far better to have earthly hopes and feelings subdued and mingled with higher ones;

that I can never forget how uncertain and perishable everything here is, and how dependent one must feel on God for every possession granted to us. Of the dearest earthly treasures any single moment may deprive us; and in the midst of the purest blessings to be enjoyed here, so much of care, of anxiety, and vexation is mingled, that nothing but constant and habitual recourse to spiritual comfort can stay the mind in perfect peace, and calm the variableness of human feelings. Surely I should be grateful for the chastening which has brought this more forcibly home, and for the links of sweet remembrance which have attended even my hours of suffering and sorrow.

To the Same.

October 24, 1828.

Anybody would, perhaps, be astonished to find me sometimes reading upon *resignation* and *afflictions* in a time of rejoicing; but the truth is, I cannot rejoice without trembling, and never felt more strongly the need of support and stay upon something not human than now, when I feel my whole soul is so engrossed with what is, and must be, so uncertain and precarious. I tremble for myself and for him. We are building upon a happiness to come, which seems so perfect, that I cannot but feel the possibility of its not being realized. In thinking of the future, it is with the earnest prayer that I may enjoy what is given me of happiness here, in subjection and complete submission to the divine will, whenever it is thought fit to deprive me of it. Whichever way I turn, I see such causes for thankfulness, that I know not how to give utterance to half that passes through my mind; at the same time, I cannot but feel the *trial* that such a tie to earth is. On this point, however, I feel sure that I cannot remain stationary with a companion such as Augustus, and that the duties opening upon me will rouse my every faculty to exertion, and be a constant call to watchfulness and attention.

To the Same.

December 22, 1832.

I hope this may reach you on Christmas Day, that it may bring us more forcibly to your mind's eye, join us more earnestly in your prayers, and communicate to you something of that share of joy we shall be feeling with you, in the coming again of that blessed season. It is a comfort to think that others are feeling it with us, and that Christmas is to many a quiet soul bringing its glad tidings, not the less surely, because it is, alas! in these times, only in secret that the real joy can often be felt. It is, indeed, sad to think that in a Christian country, and uniting as most do in Christian worship, this should be so—that the Name uppermost in our hearts should not be allowed to pass our lips, and that the *real* cause for rejoicing is the one that cannot be even hinted at. But we must not turn to the sadder side. Let us rather think of the many thousands who have, by the first coming of this day, been turned from darkness into light, and of the peace and comfort to our own hearts springing up with the assurance of a Saviour, which is Christ the Lord. . . . It is, I do believe, our little faith which chains down our thoughts to the mournful recollection of our own weakness, instead of leading them upwards to forget ourselves in the adoration of our Lord and Master, and which so prevents our feelings burning within us, and makes us serious instead of glad. When, however, we see how little there is of *peace on earth*, no wonder if we are often sad.

To the Rev. R. Kilvert.

Rome, February 6, 1834.

I scarcely know how to write to you, and can only do so in forgetting our short acquaintance, and presuming on that kind interest you have expressed towards us, and on that sympathy one Christian heart must feel for others on whom God lays His chastening hand. Mr. Hare makes no progress, and I have lately had the anguish of learning that his lungs are now decidedly affected. Under these circumstances, I try in vain to be sanguine, and though all things are possible with God, I cannot blind myself to the persuasion that it is in His eternal counsels that this His servant should be taken away from us. Augustus himself leaves all without fear and anxiety in a Father's hands, and speaks with the utmost calmness of the issue, mourning only over his own unworthiness in his Master's service. May that blessed Master, who chastens because He loves, strengthen his faith and mine, to increase his joy and hope in believing, and sustain me through the deep waters! He constantly says God gives him nothing to bear—gives him nothing but blessings; yet his cough is very bad, and his weakness increases. Your prayers, I know, will be with us, and those of all our affectionate friends at Alton; and we will pray for them also, that this and every other trial may lead them on more earnestly to seek that peace and rest which this sorrowing world can never give.

To Mrs. Edward Stanley.

February 27, 1834.

Just near the end, his anxiety seemed chiefly that I should not see him suffer. I therefore drew a little of the curtain, that he might not see me. Oh what a feeling it is, watching the departing spirit, and feeling that any moment may be the one when it takes its flight! And yet, scarcely then could self be felt—scarcely could I turn to myself, or think of anything but his release; and still now, when a whole week has passed, when every trace of him outwardly is gone, I hardly feel it so personally. We talk of him as if he were here. I have him with me so vividly, it scarcely seems possible that we are so divided; there was something in his freshness and elasticity of spirits to the very last, which, to a singular degree, prevents one's feeling that he *is not*. My dearest, dearest Augustus! It does at times come over me that I shall have him no more; that his ever bright mind is to cheer me no longer; that the perfection of earthly love is passed away; and then, when the sense of it is too strong to bear, I turn to my God—my Saviour. I feel that this world is passing, that it is but a pilgrimage, and that *the* home, that home where he is now rejoicing in glory, is the one we shall have for *ever;* and then I feel that along my path here, desolate as it now seems, there are many blessings scattered on every side to lighten and cheer it, and I may yet be able to do my Master service. There are still the poor left for me to minister to, still mourners to be comforted, many to love and to be loved by; and when my heart is very sad, if I only ask it earnestly enough, I shall still have the strength given and comfort vouchsafed, that I have had in the last few weeks of extreme need.

To Lucy A. Hare, on the First Anniversary of her Marriage.

September 24, 1834.

Shall such a day as this day pass unnoticed, dearest Luie? Do I not too well know what the 2nd of June was? Do I not too deeply feel what thankfulness I owe my Father in heaven for the blessing He gave me on this day, to let it go by without an outward expression to you, no less than a fervent prayer to Him, of all I feel and think? Oh may the union thus begun be one not for time but for eternity! As your affection one towards the other grows and deepens, may your earthly marriage be but the type of that heavenly one, when, clothed, not in your own garments, but in the fine linen of Christ's spotless righteousness, and adorned in the bridal jewels of love and holiness, you may both, at your several calls to meet the Bridegroom, be found ready, with oil in your lamps! . . . Oh how deep will be your thankfulness this day, and how your joy will be mixed with awful seriousness, in the feeling that he who so richly shared your last year's happiness, to whom this day was a consummation so earnestly desired of earthly wishes, is now transferred from grace to glory, and, in the kingdom of the blessed Jesus, is amid the saints, rejoicing tenfold in the hope that the joy he is now realizing may, through your means, be brought home to others! There are moments when "the sweetness of the stream" does give me such a foretaste of what the "fountain" must be, that I can only adore and bless my God that my beloved is now tasting all the joy and bliss, unsullied by the alloy inseparable from earthly weakness and infirmity; and the thought of his former presence and my present solitude is insufficient to check the thankfulness of my heart. . . . We are travelling on together through the same wilderness, and yet the promised land is even now open to us; the desert is even now turned into the garden of Eden; the rose blossoms, even though its thorns are not all yet broken off; and the ransomed can even now find joy and gladness, though all sorrow and all sighing are not yet at an end.

To the Same.

February 21, 1835.

"In all their affliction He was afflicted, and the angel of His presence saved them; in His love and His pity He redeemed them and bare them all the days of old." These words were my comforters on the 18th—the words with which I strove to cast off the strong and painful recollections of the last struggles of a departing spirit, and look up to Him who then in that hour of first desolation, no less than through a whole widowed year, has looked down on me and had compassion. . . . It is so blessed a privilege to *roll* all one's cares upon God; to know that He will watch over those that love Him; that not one drop will be added to the cup beyond what is wholesome and good. My song of praise on that first morning of my widowhood (Psalm cxviii. 14 to the end), has been truly mine through this year. May I be graciously permitted to sing it with increasing earnestness; to feel the "Head stone of the corner" more and more truly my Refuge and Dependence, till I may sing it in the heavenly Jerusalem, with him who is now rejoicing in all the fulness of joy! You need not fear for my health; I am creeping on by very slow degrees, and in His own good time my heavenly Father will give me such a portion of ease and comfort as He sees good for me, to do the work He has for me. May I only be faithful in His service, and count all loss but the furthering His glory, and being conformed to His image! I know now how *little* I believe, how weak is my faith, how much I lack of humility and Christian love; and I know that I can no more rest on myself for one moment than the tottering babe can let go its mother's hand. But I am ambitious! I do desire to advance far along the road I have now only entered, and to draw many along with me. Still, the flesh is weak, though the spirit is willing, and at present I can only suffer and endure.

To Miss Hibbert.

Stoke Rectory, December 24, 1834.

It is my constant grief to feel that all the strength and comfort I have is attributed to my *mental* power of exertion, whilst I am so sensible that were I for one day to have my cruse of oil unrenewed, my strength of mind would, with the present pressure on it, give way at once. Were it not for the all-sustaining arm of my Redeemer and my God, for the gracious answers He vouchsafes to my unworthy prayers, I should be weaker than the weakest; for it is always forgotten by those who so set up the natural strength of character, that along with it goes also a natural strength of feeling that requires even a greater degree of supernatural strength than a mind weaker in itself. When, when will people learn to give glory to God in the highest? My dear Letitia, I have now, as you know, been ten months in the greatest of all human afflictions; for the last five months I have been constantly ill and extremely weak; all resources of active life have been entirely cut off; my longings to benefit others—first the poor, and afterwards my own family—by leading them in the right way, have been entirely prevented, and I have been forced to give up one attempt after another at exertion both of mind and body; and yet I can most truly say that never has my abiding peace, nay, even my happiness, deserted me. "The shadow of a great rock in a weary land" has been over me. He who promised to comfort, even as a mother comforteth her child, has comforted and refreshed me. My connection, indeed, with this earth does seem altogether rent asunder, and all around me even here, where there is so much to remind me of the past, appears like a dream—a picture that I can look at, now the first shock is over, almost without emotion. My real life is that hidden one with Christ in God, which is a never-failing well-spring of delight; and though in proportion as my health enables me to return more to the usual routine of daily life and society, the struggle must be greater to preserve the spiritual joy and peace that can support me under the earthly privation, I have found constant and earnest prayer so effectual, my God so faithful, so tender in mercy and loving-kindness, that I feel as if it would be the height of ingratitude, the most inexcusable want of faith, were I for one moment to doubt that He will bear me up unto the end, and that He will never give me one trial or struggle more than is fit for me. My prevailing feeling on returning here is not how much I have suffered, but how much mercy I have received, during the last year. To have the gulf removed that separated me from God, to feel that union as of a branch in the Vine, makes all suffering appear light, since it is by His will—since by it we may be more closely conformed to His image, Who was made perfect through suffering. Were it not for this, were it not for the unspeakable joy of believing that Jesus came at this time to be *my* Saviour, to buy for me an inheritance undefiled, there where my beloved and angel one is now rejoicing before His throne; how could I bear the remembrance of those Christmas seasons we spent together at Alton, so blessed in every earthly happiness?—how could I support the recollection of last year's watching by him at Genoa? The glad tidings, mingled as they are with such thoughts, come with a chastened and sober joy; but it is such as is most meet for the waiting Christian, who has yet to bear the burden of sin, and is not yet permitted to taste fully the glory that is to be revealed. Much as it has been given me to feel of spiritual joy and love, doubtless to lighten that weight of earthly sorrow that would otherwise have been too heavy for me to bear, I feel sure the safest and surest state for one travelling along the ordinary path of life, must be one of quiet and confiding dependence upon the

Saviour's strength, and simple obedience to His will, whether of doing or suffering. I asked *earnestly* for strength to be given to me for going once more to Alton, which appeared almost impossible at the time; it was granted. From the time I besought restoration of health to enable me to get here, which had been delayed from week to week, it was given. I mention these to strengthen your faith, which you say is weak. Of course, temporal gifts must be altogether submitted to His Fatherly knowledge and wisdom; but we must not be afraid of making *all* our requests known to such a Friend.

To the Same.

Stoke, January 29, 1835.

I have this morning seen in the paper that your house is become a house of mourning. I know none of the particulars attending your affliction, and am therefore altogether ignorant of the peculiar consolations or trials with which it is accompanied. But the loss to you of a parent, to your beloved mother of a husband, is one of so serious a nature that, with the feelings of a fellow-mourner, I cannot rest till I have poured out to you something of that comfort with which I myself have been comforted. I know, indeed, most truly, how powerless human comfort is; that there is One alone who in such seasons can arise with comfort on His wings; still, the voice of a sister in sorrow, a sister in Christian hope, cannot be unacceptable. You will already have felt the exceeding mercy which allows us in such heaviness of heart to go *boldly* to the throne of grace; you are, I doubt not, daily experiencing the blessedness of that refuge from the storm provided for us in Him who was made perfect through suffering. . . . It is only, I am persuaded, by an entire and full renunciation of our own wills, a child-like submission to His loving though chastening hand, that we can find rest for our souls. And even if all appears dead and gloomy, even though there may not be that sensible comfort, that precious hope, which is sometimes vouchsafed to cheer and lighten our path of sorrow, still it is the Lord that doeth it, and most surely will He do as seemeth unto Him good. Our views are short-sighted and earthly and narrow; we see little beyond our own little world of hopes and fears, but He who is Lord of all knoweth all the breadth, and length, and depth, and height of wisdom and of love, and He will appoint all things for His glory. He can make all things work together for good to those that love Him, and will, doubtless, by means of this trial of your faith, renew your strength, and lead you to a more stedfast and abiding hope of glory. . . . I have found the greatest comfort in those passages where we are exhorted not henceforth to live to ourselves, but for Him who died and rose again; by keeping ever in mind that we are not *our own*, but bought with a price, and therefore all our aim, our desire, our joy, should be to glorify God with body and spirit, since they are *God's, not ours*. When I am tempted to faint at the thoughts of the dreariness of life, it may be many years of life, it is an unfailing source of comfort to dwell on the thought that here I am to suffer God's will, that *He* may be glorified; that my own ease and pleasure are not to be looked at for one moment; and that by conformity to the life and mind of Christ, if through the gracious means He Himself gives us, I am able to further the salvation of one soul, the present chastening even now appears rather joyous than grievous. A thousand years in His sight are but as a day. Hereafter, they will appear as such to us too. Let us, then, forget what is behind, and reach on to what is before, remembering that each trial is a *trust,* for which we have to answer. It is the voice of God speaking to our souls of things to come, and warning us to leave things below. May we never rest contented with our present hope; but let us go on day by day, growing in grace and in the knowledge of our Lord Jesus, firmly assured that *whatsoever* we ask of Him, if it be according to His will, we shall certainly receive. He is ever the same, as ready to hear to-day as He was yesterday, as abundant in grace to-morrow as to-day. May He heal all your sorrows, strengthen your faith, and quicken your love! prays your affectionate fellow-mourner and sister in Christ.

To Miss Clinton.

March, 1839.

In my continued weakness, I find that it is good to be kept constantly in mind that the ways in which one would like best to serve God are not always the ways in which He chooses one should show one's love and readiness to do His will. "To stand and wait" is a harder task to flesh and blood than "to speed o'er land and ocean without rest," and if the exercise serves to school one into perfect submission, it is a blessed one, for which one should be thankful. To be useless to others, when one fancies one might be able to do them good; to give no pleasure, when one longs to comfort or please; to be from bodily infirmity unable to share the enjoyment of others; and show one's light-heartedness, though inwardly full of joy and peace; these are the constant thwartings of one's own will, that may work out good in a way we see not, and, doubtless, since ordained by God, will not tend to lessen His glory, though we may wish it had been in our power to advance it in our own way.

To Mrs. R. Pile.

April 24, 1840.

Whether there is a feeling of joy and rest in our hearts, matters not, if we feel resolute in *doing* the will of God. If you find a slackness in this wish of devoting yourself and all you have to His service, then lose no time, but go and pour out your heart before Him, tell Him all your deadness and weakness, and leave not wrestling in prayer till He gives you a more earnest desire to follow Him. So many Christians, I think, go on in needless despondency and depression from not *at once*, when they feel lifeless towards God, going to lay their burden on Him who will bear it for them, and in return will assuredly impart His righteousness. . . . You have, no doubt, a great deal to do and think of that is of the earth, earthy; try and lift this very business into heavenly places, by doing it with the Spirit of Christ. You are serving Him often quite as acceptably, quite as faithfully, when engaged in your earthly calling, as when reading His Word, or on your knees in prayer. At the same time, it is necessary to go apart occasionally to ask specially for help and grace to be able to do this, and it is surprising how few minutes of your time it would take, if you would redeem this little time for your God. Often, when I have lamented over not having *more time* for communion with Him, it has quite humbled me to find, on looking at my watch, that when I have, as I thought, made an effort to give up my time to this purpose, the utmost duration has been, perhaps, *ten minutes*. I mention this as an encouragement to feel how little real cause we have to excuse ourselves from prayer on account of *want of time;* at the same time that it may deeply humble one to feel how slack one's heart is thus to speak to God.

R

To Lucy A. Hare.

April 30, 1841.

Is your sea as exquisitely blue as this; and have you been enjoying the sight of it from your terraces and rocks, and trying to lift up your darlings' hearts and minds to Him who sitteth above, to us invisible, or dimly seen in these His lowest works? So Augustus* and I have been fancying to ourselves as we have walked about, and I sat down in the garden, with true May warmth and beauty all around us, the joyous birds singing their praises to God, and "all things that breathe" giving Him thanks far better than our poor thankless souls. The fields and hedgerows are now quite lined with primroses, and the copses are one sea of bluebells; and how the sight of all the flowers and the songs of the nightingales seem to take away all cares from one's mind! . . . Yet how true it is, usually, that when outward things seem prospering, one never can rejoice but in trembling! And it is good so to be; for is it not when the shadow of a cloud hangs over our earthly atmosphere, that the sun of the Heavenly One shines brightest, and our gaze is most fixed there?

To the Same.

May 14, 1841.

To-day is a day perfectly lovely. Alone here in this peaceful nook, with the cloudless vault of

---

* A nephew, adopted as her own child.

heaven above one, and the sweet, new-mown grass withering at our feet, and the thousand birds warbling in our ears, and bright flowers around, there seems nothing to separate one from God but one's poor body, that clogs and fetters the bound of one's soul upwards. He does seem so near; and when one can lay hold of one fixed thought of Him, and really feel that this outward world, lovely and beautiful as it is, is but the shadow of Him in whom is perfect *light* and never-ending *life*, oh how it does fill one's heart with joy and love while it lasts! But then comes the needful work of the day, its consequent fatigue and irritation of body, and "Where is that mighty joy that just now took up all my heart?" becomes the question. Poor mortals that we are! Well, the time will come when this mortal will put on immortality, and the joy will be full and unchanging, face to face, eye to eye, with Him at whose right hand are pleasures for evermore.

To the Same.

June 3, 1843.

Did you see the eclipse on Friday night? It could not have been a better, clearer night for it; and what an awful thing it is, even when we know the cause! It gives one a shudder to think that the light of the Sun of Righteousness could thus be blotted out from His Church, and instead of being "fair as the moon," it should be left to its native darkness; for it is truly only by a borrowed light that we can shine, and the earth is ever seeking to overshadow us, and hide us from the true light. It began here at 9.10, and when I went to bed at ten o'clock it was blood-red; and from my bed I could see it perfectly till the silvery light again returned, and the dark shade moved away. It made one feel so what God must be, who thus acts and moves the universe; and how near He is; and that such signs in heaven will probably attend the day when the Son of man is revealed, "The sun shall be darkened, and the moon shall not give her light."

I have had much comfort lately in meditating on the passages which show the personality of the Holy Ghost, and His distinctness from the Father and the Son. It is a subject that requires searching into to find out, but, when realized, gives one so much more true and lively a sense of the fulness of the Godhead, and its work in us and to us, than when only thinking of the Spirit in its effect on us. What unsearchable riches there are in the Word of God!—a mine, into which the deeper we dig, the more unfathomable it is found.

To the Same.

September 30, 1845.

May you enjoy the rest of your stay in your blessed though widowed home; and may all your hallowed thoughts and recollections there fit you for living on in every place wheresoever you are, keeping close to Him who is ever present and near! and in

Him you will ever be with your own Marcus. Yesterday, in thinking of the "angels and archangels, and all the glorious company of heaven," how one did feel that all one desired was to share their work of fulfilling the will of God while on earth, that one might share their joy in heaven! Some foretaste, some glimpses of that joy, are vouchsafed us in seasons of our greatest need, to encourage us onward; but here below we are not called to dwell on Mount Tabor, but must return after a while to show what Jesus has done for us, and to accomplish His good pleasure. It is only when patience has had its perfect work that we may hope to rest from our labours, and enjoy for evermore the fulness of pleasure and love and holiness.

To the Same.

October 5, 1845.

I fear your outer shell will be much worn this week; but in the midst of outward toil and trouble, there will ever be the inward peace which exists in God—the Rock that cannot be moved. I do feel for you in leaving your precious home, and the desolateness of going forth alone; but as you are getting through your work, you will steal a little time to spend in communion with the unseen world, and to find strength for looking above things temporal, and finding rest for your spirit in Him who changes not. And, while feeling painfully how changed the outward scene will be, and that those memorials to which you cling so fondly will be removed from your sight, you will, when you draw near to Jesus, feel that He is in all places the same ever-present Friend and Saviour, and that in His sight you can dwell in the fullest communion with him who has entered beyond the vail, where the Lord is his everlasting Light. . . . We also are travelling on there, and what does it matter if the way be tedious and painful at times; it is so *sure,* so certain, that we shall get home after a while, and then no storms from without or within can touch us? I feel quite impatient under writing to you now, when I hope so soon to have you dwelling with me, and talking together of all we love best, cheering each other in the heavenly road, not looking back, but gathering strength to look onward. May the Lord comfort your heart, and strengthen your frail body!

To the Same.

February 18, 1867.

I have been reading the life of Mrs. Mary Fletcher, the saintly wife of the saintly man, Mr. Fletcher of Madeley. And in her sufferings at his death, after only four years of blessed union, there is much to recall those of my own past, now thirty-three years ago. Since that sad day, in 1834, many waves have rolled over me, but truly can I say that through all I have been upheld by the mercy of my God. I always think the continual exhortation to the Israelites to "remember" what the Lord had done for them, is a lesson to us to let past mercies be a ground of hope for the future. The time will come, dearest, when we shall wonder we could ever doubt or fear, and still more how we could for our poor aims sin against Him. So let us take courage and go on our way, till we are with those who have gone before us into the presence-chamber, and see as we are seen; though till then we must have much, both within and without, to sadden our spirits.

SARA COLERIDGE.

XV.

SARA COLERIDGE, daughter of SAMUEL TAYLOR COLERIDGE, was born in 1802; married her cousin, HENRY NELSON COLERIDGE, in 1829; and lived eighteen years after her husband's death in 1843, dying in 1851.

TO HER MOTHER.

October 24, 1836.

I entreat you to pray for cheerfulness and fortitude to the Giver of all good. Be sure that the effort to pray will be useful, however distracted your poor thoughts may be. Let us recollect, that were we enjoying all that our worldly hearts desire, how rapidly time moves on; how soon shall we arrive at the end of our earthly course! then what will worldly good things avail us? But these days of trial are more available for securing a happy seat in the eternal kingdom, than those which our unsanctified hearts might deem more blessed. The merciful Saviour has given us a check in the midst of our heedless career, and bids us consider, ere it be too late, whither we are hastening; but we think only of the roses on the wayside, and forget the glorious city in the clouds, which, would we raise our eyes, we might see right before us. Dearest mother, be not grieved for this visitation. When you go to heaven before me, if you leave your poor daughter with a more serious, chastened heart (though still a weak and sin-inclined one), you leave her in far better case than if her frame were as free from uneasy weakness as the best in the land. Look not on this as a poor consolation, only taken up because no better can be had. These which I have alluded to are substantial truths, which will abide to my weal or woe, when all this busy, bustling world for me exists no longer. I thought my business here was to teach my darling boy; to be respected, admired, beloved; my head said otherwise, but my heart felt thus. Now I feel more feelingly that my business here is to make my soul fit for eternity, and my earthly tasks are but the means by which that blessed work of my salvation is to be effected. Not according to what I do here, but according to the spirit in which I do it, shall I be judged hereafter. Is there anything in this reflection that tends to weaken our zeal, prudence, industry, forecast in the exercise of our earthly avocations? Our worldly things would be better done than they are, could we but view them only in their due relation to heavenly things; as children are best educated when they are accounted as children, and not treated with the state and ceremony and indulgence that rightly belong to the mature. God bless you, my beloved mother.

Extract from a Letter to Miss Burke.

September 8, 1838.

It is but few, perhaps, who have time to acquire any clear or systematic knowledge of divinity. When the heart is right, individuals may be in some respects first-rate Christians without any speculative insight, because the little time for study is caused by active exertion; and this active exertion, pursued in a religious spirit, and converted into the service of God by the way of performing it, is, perhaps, the most effective school of Christianity. But when there *is* time to read, then I do think that, both for the sake of others and of ourselves, the cultivation of the intellect, with a view to religious knowledge, is a positive duty.

To Mrs. Stanger.

August 10, 1840.

Your last kind note was written in a strain which harmonized well with my feelings. Would that those feelings, which a trial such as we have lately sustained must needs bring with it to all who have learned, in any degree, however insufficient, to trust in Heaven, whether for temporary consolation or for eternal happiness,—would that those feelings could be more lasting than they are; that they could leave strong and permanent traces; that they could become the *very habit* of our souls, not a mere mood or passing state, without any settled foundation! My thoughts had turned the same way as yours, where all mourners and friends of those that mourn will naturally go for sure and certain hope and ground of rejoicing, to that most divine chapter of the raising of Lazarus. "Thy brother shall rise again." ... Our loss, indeed, has been a great disappointment, and even a sorrow; for, strange as it may seem, these little speechless creatures, with their wandering, unspeaking eyes, do twine themselves round a parent's heart from the hour of their birth.

On her Husband's Illness.

December, 1842.

I try to think of that better abode in which we may meet with each other, free from those ills which flesh is heir to. We have a special need to look and long for the time when we may be clothed upon " with our house which is from heaven"; for in this tabernacle we do, indeed, groan, " being burdened." Bodily weakness and disorder have been the great (and only) drawbacks, ever since we met twenty years ago, to our happiness in each other. It will seem chimerical to you that I have not yet abandoned *all* hope. But this faint hope, which, perhaps, however, is stronger than I imagine, does not render me unprepared for what all around me expect. The Lord has given; and when He takes away, I can resign him to his Father in heaven; and, looking in that direction in which he will have gone, I shall be able to have that peace and comfort which in no shape then will the world be able to give me.

On the Same.

January, 1843.

I now feel quite happy, or at least satisfied. Could I arrest his progress to a better sphere of existence by a prayer, I would not utter it. When I once know that it *is* God's will, I can feel that it is right, even if there were no definite assurances of rest and felicity beyond this world. I cannot be too thankful to God, so far as my own best interests are concerned, that He is thus removing from earth to heaven my greatest treasure while I have strength and probably time to benefit by the measure, and learn to look habitually above; which now will not be the spirit against the flesh, but both pulling one way, for the heart will follow the treasure. Thus graciously does the blessed Jesus condescend to our infirmities, by earthly things leading us to heavenly ones.

To the Rev. H. Moore, after her Husband's Death.

February 13, 1843.

I must pen two or three lines to thank you for your last letter, and to tell you that I accept from my heart all your offers of friendship to me and mine. When I call your letter "most brotherly," with such brothers as I have, it is the strongest epithet that I can use. . . . But in this mingled cup there are other sorrows of a still deeper kind; for physical evil is not *evil* in the most real sense.

The separation is a fearful wrench from one for whom, and in expectation of whose smile, I might almost say, I have done all things, even to the choice of the least article of my outward apparel, for twenty years. But even that is not the heaviest side of the dispensation; it is to feel not merely that he is taken from me, but that, as *appears*, though it is appearance, he is not; that the sun rises in the morning, and he does not see it. The higher, and better, and enduring mind within us has no concern with these sensations, but they *will* arise, and have a certain force. While we remain in the tabernacle of the flesh, they are the miserable cloggy vapours that from time to time keep steaming up from the floor and walls, and obscure the prospect of the clear empyrean which may be seen from the windows. The most effective relief from them which I have found, is the reminding myself that he who has passed from my sight is gone whither I myself look to go in a few years (not to mention all those of whom the world was not worthy, before the publication of the gospel, and since); and that if I can contemplate my own removal, not with mere calmness, but with a cheerfulness which no other thought bestows, why should I feel sad that he is there before me? But these of which I have spoken are only the sensations of the natural man and woman. I well know in my heart of hearts, and better mind, that if he is not now in the bosom of God, who is not the God of the dead, but of the living; or if all these hopes are but dreams,—I can have but little wish to bring him back to earth again, or to care about anything, either in earth or heaven. In my weakest moments, indeed, I have never wished that it were possible to recall him, or to prevent his departure hence? I thank God and the power of His grace that there has been no agony in my grief, there has been no struggle of my soul with Him. I have always had such a strong sense and conviction that if this sorrow *was to be*, and was appointed by God, it was entirely right, and that it was mere senselessness to wish anything otherwise than as infinite goodness and infinite wisdom had ordained it.

To Miss Morris, in answer to a Letter, containing an Account of a Crushing Sorrow, by Death from Accident, in the Writer's Family, and of the Christian Resignation with which it was borne.

October 6, 1847.

Most sincerely do I thank you for your letter, which affected me deeply—affects me, I may say, for I cannot look at it, or think of it, without feeling my eyes fill with tears. It contains a record which will ever be precious to me, a testimony to the power of faith, one of those testimonies which makes us feel with special force that Christianity is no mere speculation or subject of abstract thought, but a blessed and glorious reality—the *only* reality, to speak by comparison. But I believe it impossible for us in this earthly sphere to realize religion without an attendant process of destruction. While this destruction of the natural goes on within us gradually, we do not notice it; but in great affliction, when much work is done at once, the disruption is strongly felt; and the body for a time gives way. After a while, even the body seems to gain new strength; it has adjusted itself to a new condition of the soul; it remains attenuated, but firm. We seem to have passed into a partly new state of existence, a stage of the new birth. One coat of worldliness has been cast off; the natural is weaker and slenderer within us, and the spiritual larger and stronger. I seem to myself scarce worthy to talk of such things. I have not profited by affliction as I ought to have done. Better than I once was, possessed of a far deeper sense of the beauty and excellence of Christianity, I do humbly hope that I am. But I have had, perhaps, too much worldly support—*earthly* support, I should rather say. Things of the mind and intellect give me intense pleasure; they delight and amuse me, as they are in themselves, independently of aught they can introduce me to instrumentally; and they have gladdened me in another way, by bringing me into closer communion with fine and deep minds. It has seemed a duty, for my children's sake and my own, to cultivate this source of cheerfulness, and, sometimes, I think, the result has been too *large*, the harvest too abundant, of inward satisfaction. This is dangerous. How hardly shall the rich man enter into the kingdom of heaven! And these are the richest of earthly riches. They who *use* intellect as the means of getting money and reputation, are drudges, poor slaves— though even they have often a high pleasure in the means, while they are pursuing an unsatisfactory end. But they who live in a busy, yet calm world of thought and poetry, though their *powers* may be far less that those of the others, may forget heaven, if sorrow and sickness and symptoms of final decay, do not force them to look up, and strive away from their little transitory heaven upon earth to that which is above. Bright, indeed, that little heaven continually is with light from the Supernal One. But we rest too content with these *reflections*, which must fade as our mortal frame loses power. Hope of a higher existence can alone support us when this half-mental, half-bodily happiness declines.

To Miss Fenwick.

May 6, 1850.

I shall be thankful to see any letters from Rydal that you can forward. How dear Mrs. Wordsworth is to bear the trial of separation, and parting sorrow, and fatigue undergone in the last illness, is, perhaps, yet to appear. I trust we may augur well from the long-prepared state of her mind, and her living faith in the resurrection and our reunion with departed friends. Still, in some respects, the more we dwell upon that prospect, the more we strive to realize it, the deeper is the trial to our weak bodily frame. We know that another state of existence must be far other than this; that a spiritual world cannot be like an earthly world. We cannot penetrate the shades that hang over the state of souls after their departure. The subject that is spoken of under the name of the "intermediate state," of this what brief notices we have, and how ambiguous! How the best and wisest men differ about the interpretation of them! The more we think of the state after death, the deeper is the awe with which we must contemplate it; and, sometimes, in weakness, we long for the happy, bright imaginations of childhood, when we saw the other world vividly pictured, a bright and perfect copy of the world in which we live, with sunshine and flowers, and all that constituted our earthly enjoyment! In after years, we strive to translate these images into something higher. We say, all this we shall have, but in some higher form; "Flesh and blood cannot inherit the kingdom of God, neither doth corruption inherit incorruption." All this beauty around us is perishable; its outward form and substance is corruption, but there is a soul in it, and *this* shall rise again; and so our beloved friends that are removed, we shall see them again, but changed—altered into what we now cannot conceive or image, with celestial bodies fit for a celestial sphere.

Part of a Letter written a Short Time before her Death.

October 1, 1851.

Oh, this life is very dear to me! The outward beauty of earth, and the love and sympathy of fellow-creatures, make it, to my feelings, a sort of heaven half-ruined—an Elysium, into which a dark, tumultuous ocean is perpetually rushing, to agitate and destroy, to lay low the blooming flowers of tranquil bliss, and drown the rich harvests. Love is the sun of this lower world; and we know from the beloved disciple that it will be the bliss of heaven. God is love, and whatever there may be that we cannot now conceive, love will surely be contained in it. It will be love sublimed, and incorporated in beauty, infinite and perfect. I am very weak and faint to-day—more so than I have yet been; but I have been as low in nerves formerly; otherwise I might think that I had entered into the Dark Valley, and was approaching the River of Death. How kind of Bunyan—what a beneficent imagination!—to shadow out death as a *river*, which is so pleasant to the mind, and carries it on into regions bright and fair, beyond that boundary stream!

ROBERT GRAY.

XVI.

ROBERT GRAY was born in 1809, ordained in 1833, appointed Vicar of Whitworth in 1834, Vicar of Stockton-on-Tees 1845, consecrated Bishop of Cape Town 1847, and died in 1872.

To Dr. WILLIAMSON, ON BEING ASKED IF HE WOULD BE LIKELY TO ACCEPT THE BISHOPRIC OF EITHER ADELAIDE OR THE CAPE.

1847.

I enclose you a letter received yesterday, which is causing me much anxiety and trouble of mind. I send it for your consideration and opinion, and shall feel thankful if you will give them to me candidly and decidedly. So many and such weighty considerations are involved in a decision on the subject, that I tremble to make the attempt. Of course, it presents itself to my mind under a variety of aspects. What I want you to give me your opinion upon is—first, as to my fitness for the office. My conviction is that in many, very many, important qualifications I am utterly deficient. Indeed, I know of none that I possess, except a kind of brute energy, and a certain amount of success in influencing others so as to lead them to co-operate with me. In learning, judgment, talent, temper, piety, I feel I am far below what such an office requires. In each of the colonies named, the Church is *nothing;* everything has to be done. . . . I own it has always appeared to me that the *first* bishop of a colonial see should have qualifications which I have no pretensions to. Then, next, supposing your opinion to be that I am fit for such an office, do you think me, before God, at liberty to decline it? My own belief is that a man is bound to go where he will be most likely to promote the glory of God, the good of His Church, and the salvation of souls. If I know myself, I think I am prepared in this matter to go, or not to go, just as God would have me do. If I could see my way *clearly,* in point of *duty,* I would act accordingly. I wish to come to a decision without reference to personal considerations. Will you, then, secondly, if you think me qualified, tell me what you think *I ought* to do under the circumstances? Then, thirdly, let me know whether you agree or differ with me as to not being influenced by temporal considerations. Were I convinced that there was no call of duty, that I had a perfect freedom of choice, that I was not shrinking from a divine call, I think I should decline. Home attachments, wife, children, comfort in present sphere of duty, would all combine to keep me here. Humanly speaking, my heart would sink within me at the thoughts of what I should have to encounter, as it were, alone, in either of those spiritually desolate regions; at the vast responsibility of the office itself. The carrying away, too, from all she holds dear, of my most self-denying, devoted, high-minded wife, to the very antipodes of the earth; the education and worldly prospects of my children; all these, even now, crowd upon my mind overpoweringly, and would, I think, deter me, were there no counter-feeling that I might be refusing to hearken when God was calling. Give me your prayers, and your advice. I am at a loss how to act. But I *think* of saying that if the archbishop has before him a list of men well qualified for the office, or if Hawkins knows of men who would be fit and willing to go, I had rather not have it offered me. But that if otherwise—if those whom they deem competent are unwilling to go, and others cannot easily be found, I place myself at the disposal of the Church.

To the Rev. Ernest Hawkins.

1847.

I have had some difficulty in making up my mind as to the answer which I ought to send to your letter of the 30th January. If I know myself, I believe I have wished to be guided simply by convictions of duty. Could I have seen my way clearly in the matter, and felt satisfied that there was a call from Divine Providence, I should have been ready to decide at once to go anywhere, and in any situation. But upon this point I have had very conflicting feelings, and very considerable doubts. There is no need, however, that I should trouble you with an account of what has been passing in my mind. I shall, therefore, content myself with saying that after consulting the bishop, my brothers, and one or two friends, I wish to leave the matter thus: That if from your position you know, or have reason to think, that the archbishop has before him, or you are prepared to lay before him, the names of other men whom you deem equally qualified for the office, I had rather not be named. But if there is really a dearth of men who are both competent and willing to undertake it, I would place myself at the disposal of the Church; for I think, in that case, I ought not to shrink from what might then appear a plain duty. . . . I have no wish whatever to go, but I am willing to obey any call of God.

To the Archbishop of Canterbury.

March 9, 1847.

I only received your grace's letter by this day's post, though dated the 6th. Considering all the circumstances of the case, I do not think that I should feel justified in declining to accede to your grace's proposal. It seems to me that in doing so I should be shrinking from the call of God. I therefore readily and cheerfully place myself at the disposal of the Church, and am prepared to obey your grace's summons to occupy the post of a missionary bishop at the Cape. It shall be my unwearied endeavour to promote the glory of God, and the welfare of His Church, in that important colony to which I am about to be sent. But no one can feel so keenly as myself my utter inability adequately to discharge the duties of that office, from which I have shrunk as long as I have felt liberty to do so, but which I no longer decline to undertake, now that your grace, knowing what my feelings are, sees fit to press it upon me.

To Dr. Williamson.

October, 1848.

Our Church is, indeed, in a sad condition. . . . There is that to be done and undone which is sufficient to break the spirit and wear out the energies of better men than myself. But I will not write despondingly; it would be sinful. God is, I trust, with us. Much has already been done in this land to place things on a better footing, and the hearts of men are cheered. Things have, too, in many ways fallen out wonderfully for the furtherance of the gospel. I attribute much to the prayers of those who are dear to me; and it is a great comfort to me, and gives me much confidence, to know that many daily intercede for us.

To the Rev. Henry Gray.

April, 1849.

How rapidly life is passing on! May we, my dear brother, each be preparing for eternity! The wrench which separated me from home, and so many who are dear; and the many calls of duty which compel me to become a wanderer upon earth, away from dearest wife and children; do, I think, contribute to wean me from the world, and make me, I trust, more alive to things eternal. Certainly, except for the sake of wife and little ones, I have no desire to live one day longer than I may be useful in advancing Christ's cause and kingdom upon earth; and I often think that this will not be very long, for my capacity for the great work which lies before a bishop in this diocese falls so very far short of what is needed, that I am at times much distressed to find myself in the very responsible position in which I am placed. However, for some of the very rough work which a first bishop must go through, which requires no extraordinary gifts, but physical power and energy, I have, perhaps, some little qualification; and a sense of this, together with a recollection of the way in which I shrank from the office which was really thrust upon me, often consoles me amidst a growing sense of incompetency and insufficiency. I trust you will continue to pray for me, for I need such support, and I daily feel that the prayers of God's people help me on my way.

To the Same.

July 14, 1849.

Cares and anxieties thicken here, and I am sadly wanting in that faith which can commit all to God in cheerful confidence, convinced that He will take care of His own cause. I ought to feel perfectly satisfied that all things will work together for the good of His Church here, and I do feel in the main assured of this. But each trouble, as it springs up daily in my path, is allowed to disturb and distress me in a way it should not do, and it is astonishing how thick they come upon me. I trust, my dear Henry, you will give me the benefit of your prayers, that God's cause may not suffer through my fault. Let that but prosper, and I care not for myself.

To John R. Mowbray, Esq.

July, 1850.

Though I can read but little in my present wanderings, and hear less of the Church at home, I take as deep an interest as ever in all that is passing; and I do not cease to pray that God's Holy Spirit may ever be with her, and guide her into all truth, aiding her in this her hour of trouble and rebuke, and supplying to her what is wanting in her. Earnestly do I hope that no spirit of impatience or distrust of God's mercy and love towards her, may prevent her sounder members from combining heartily, courageously, and perseveringly, for a redress of her many grievances. These must be content to witness for God's truth and cause, without being over-anxious as to the result. Let us be satisfied with doing our duty, and leave the rest to God. . . . There are nearly one million heathen within this diocese under British government or influence. We *must* have an extensive mission amongst them. I do believe that nowhere is there a more important work lying before the Church. . . . God helping, we will no longer endure the reproach of being almost the only one of the twenty religious communities in this land that is holding back from the work of the conversion of the heathen. I feel much my long absence from dearest wife and children. But it is for God's work that I leave them, and therefore I am content.

To his Son, at School in England.

January, 1855.

It is a comfort to me, dear, to be consulted by you on religious points. I can hardly, at this distance, and without knowing more of your state of mind, and daily life and conduct, say whether I think you do well or not to communicate weekly. My impression is that there will be some danger of your viewing too familiarly, if not irreverently, the most solemn act, the great mystery, of religion. A weekly communicant should be living up to a very high standard of Christian life. If you are doing this, and preparing yourself previously by much thought and self-inquiry, and wish to communicate weekly, I think you may do so, and that you will draw down many blessings upon your soul. But if you are doing it because you think the masters expect it, and will think the worse of you if you do not, or because it is the custom of others to do so, or because you think it will please me, I advise you not to do so. Of course, I should be very glad if you had a real desire for it, and found the fulness of the blessing of so doing; but to do it from any other consideration than a real belief that it was good for you, and a longing for it, would not be right or profitable. You see, therefore, that I wish to throw you upon yourself, with only a few hints to guide your judgment. I can't help thinking that you may be doing it, more from an idea that it is expected of you, than on any other ground. Write and tell me whether this is so, and give me your views on the matter. What I want you to learn to do is—to do what *you* think right, not what you think others think right for you to do. Ask yourself, when others—especially other boys—ask you to do things, whether God would have you do them. Be guided by what you think would be His will, and you will not go far wrong.

To the Same.

July, 1855.

I do not want you to think it necessary to write to me directly about your spiritual state. Nothing would shock or pain me more than an unreal religious letter. You know it would be pure hypocrisy, and as injurious to you as hateful to me. But I should like, my dearest child, that you should still, though far away from me, tell me of your feelings, and of your aspirations after good. I do not want that we should become strangers to each other; and nothing will more tend to check that than the endeavour to keep up a perfectly free and confidential intercourse. Do not scruple, therefore, to

T

tell me freely of faults and shortcomings, or to ask for counsel. I should like you from time to time to tell me whether you keep up *earnest* private prayer; whether you read Holy Scripture by yourself, and other good books, and what books, with a view to your personal improvement; whether you communicate weekly or monthly, and whether you reap the blessing of communion, or whether, through lack of earnestness, it is withheld. I desire, my dearest boy, to see you advancing in your studies, but I look with infinitely deeper interest and anxiety to your growth in faith and godliness. Make these your chief aim. Other things are desirable; these are essential. If spared to meet again, let me find you a really Christian lad. It is this that I long and pray for, more than any other thing for you.

To the Same.

June 16, 1860.

I hope you stand up for the right against the wrong, for God against the devil. There is one further point upon which you invite my opinion—the observance of Sunday. I do not think that your description of yours is altogether a satisfactory one. To a walk on Sunday I see no objection; I think it desirable; and a country walk preferable to sauntering about town. But sixteen or twenty miles, and a lunch at a wayside inn, cannot but occupy the greater part of the day. I do not think that that is a desirable, or even a lawful, way of spending it, and I am very doubtful whether you have any right to frequent an inn, when provision is already made in college for food. Surely great exertion in the week makes much Sunday exercise less, and not more necessary, as you suppose. What, however, strikes me most in your way of putting the case is this, that you contend for the utmost latitude and indulgence, if it is not positively sinful; and you sail very near the wind indeed in deciding for yourself what is right or wrong. Now this sort of temper will lead a man on further and further; the more he takes the more he will wish to take, and think it not wrong to take, and gradually his mind and judgment become warped. I do not think your Sunday calculated (as I believe Sunday occupations are intended to do) to deepen your religious convictions, and strengthen your spiritual life, but the reverse. And I think that your whole tone will be lowered and not raised, if you continue to give up so large a portion of that day to mere amusement. My view is that that is specially your day for theological work, and that if the University sermon is the only sermon you hear, you are bound to read some practical work, as, *e.g.*, Thomas à Kempis, the best of devotional books after the Bible. . . . Now you will think that I have written you more of a sermon than a letter, but the points touched upon in your letters are very important, and I am sure that you would wish me to tell you exactly what I think. I do it not with a view to find fault, but to help you.

To the Same.
October, 1863.

I suppose by this time you are just going up for your examination. . . . This work over, and a little recreation had on the Continent or elsewhere, you must begin to grapple with the great work of life. . . . The physical contests have had their place; the intellectual, too, have had their chance; the spiritual must now be entered upon. Read St. Paul's allusions to the Isthmian games, and try to realize with him the words, "Now they do it to obtain a corruptible crown, but we an incorruptible." Set this before you steadily for the rest of life. Hitherto, you have been training the lower faculties of man—the flesh, the intellect. The higher must now have the chief share of time and thought. It is with the moral and spiritual nature that man can best serve God and his fellow-men. Graces will do more than gifts for the lifting up of ourselves and others nearer to God. Now is the time when mere study has ceased to have a paramount claim on you, that the great objects for which man lives, or ought to live, should be pondered, and resolutions formed of giving yourself up wholly to God, and to His service.

To the Same.
November, 1864.

My dearest Boy,

By the time this reaches you, you will, I trust, have become a minister of Christ. From henceforth you devote yourself, soul and body, all you have and all you are, to Him and to His service. He is to be Master, you servant. For His sake, out of love to Him, you are to strive with all your might, to spread His truth and His kingdom, and win His redeemed to Him. You pledge yourself to sacrifice tastes, wishes, inclinations, prospects, all that the world has to offer, to Him—count them all as dung, if you may win Him, and be found in *that* day in Him. It is a blessed service. I would not, with all its anxieties, distresses, reproaches—and I have had my share of these—exchange it for *any* the world has to offer. Henceforth, dearest boy, you will be a fellow-labourer with your father, it may be in far distant lands, in the Lord's vineyard. May He give you grace to fight a good fight, and of His goodness to win a crown! Be true and faithful; hold to the faith once for all delivered. Witness for Christ, and you shall have a cross to bear, but He whom you serve will support and strengthen and comfort you under its burden. . . . May the life of God within your soul be deepened hour by hour!

To the Same.

July, 1865.

You say truly that there is great danger of self forcing itself into all our work, of mistaking natural activity for spiritual zeal and devotion. With you I believe that energy of character makes you throw yourself into your work with vigour. The danger would be of zeal flagging after the novelty and freshness have worn off. At first, the newness of the field and of the work interests and excites—the trial comes when it is stale and disheartening. Then, if the soul looks up to God, there come support and freshness of spirit. Your real usefulness and your perseverance will depend upon your spiritual state, so cultivate the inner life.

To Dr. Williamson, on hearing of his Failing Health.

August, 1863.

I write a few lines, after a long day, on the eve of my departure, being much grieved by the accounts just received of your difficulty in breathing, and great weakness. It may be, my dear brother, that the Master is calling you home, when we had fondly hoped to see you and hear you again holding forth the Word of Life, in that house which you have restored, in some measure, to its former beauty. If this be so, you will be the first to say, "It is the Lord, let Him do what seemeth Him good." And, dearest Annie will bow in meek submission, though you well know with a heart how near to breaking. I have clung to the hope of your sudden recovery as long as I dared. I fear that I must give up the hope, though I will yet trust and pray that you may have relief. May God comfort, support, bless you both. It is something to be able to look forward to the future, as you can do, with calm confidence, and the blessed assurance of a glorious immortality. May we meet in a brighter and happier world, if we meet no more here! I have yet to struggle in the trenches, or, like the builders of the temple, to fight with one hand, while seeking to lay the foundations of God's house with the other.

To his Sister, at the Same Time.

Your note just received, filled me with much pain, more for you than my dear Richard. The distress of looking upon one so dear drawing each breath with pain, and the thought that the slight disease was assuming a more formidable appearance, must have been very trying. But then you have ever lived in the presence of God, and know that beneath you are the everlasting arms. Perfect love casteth out fear, and speaks inward peace, and I am much mistaken if you are not feeling sweetest consolation as you look calmly to the future. There is before you both the assurance that you shall see your Lord's face in glory, and be made partakers in the fulness of the blessing of the redemption which He hath wrought. How very soon you will both share in the rest that shall never end! My heart and thoughts will be much with you both, and my prayers be offered for you. It may be your Father's purpose to spare your dear one a little longer, or to take him away. While spared, I trust that his sufferings will not be great. What marvellous ways does God work in! All that we have been mourning over in the silence of the last two years, has been His method of disciplining and training a soul for His kingdom. I trust, too, that all is being blessed to you, and aiding in perfecting you for the life that shall know no end.

T. G. RAGLAND.

XVII.

T. G. RAGLAND was born in 1815, elected Fellow of Corpus Christi College, Cambridge, in 1840. He was ordained in 1841, and worked as a curate in Cambridge till 1845. He then went to India as a missionary, and died, rather suddenly, in 1858.

Corpus Christi College, Cambridge, July 30, 1840.

If I were only to tell you my feelings of the last five weeks, with the exception of the last few days, I should have nothing to tell you of but daily and hourly mercies, and as much happiness as ever I have had for the same space of time; not in any success in reading (as you may imagine, from what I have just written), neither from any particular pleasure, more than usual, in the society of my friends here, but from God's mercy in keeping me in a spirit more contented and humble than usual, and in giving me a little more desire to glorify Him. I am sorry, however, that I cannot at present say as much about myself, but can only hope that the same may be restored to me again. I hope that I have still your prayers to help me in my course; for I find a very little sufficient to upset good resolutions and happy prospects.

Corpus Christi College, Cambridge, June 2, 1845.

My dear Mr. Venn,

I have been thinking, ever since our meetings, a fortnight since, about the great want of men to go out as missionaries to the heathen; and after deep consideration and much prayer, and consulting of a few decided Christian friends, I write to you, in the hope that you, my dear sir, will kindly give me your advice and prayers to help me to discover what is my duty in this matter. I think, as far as I know my own heart, that I am willing to go out as a missionary, if I could only see good reason to believe that such is the will of God. I feel, too, the more I think upon the subject, my desire towards the work is increased rather than diminished. I am aware of the wrong motives, of some of them at least, which I am in danger of being swayed by, and of these *especially* the desire of being well spoken of by the Church at home. After, however, having endeavoured to extricate my heart from the influence of these wrong motives, I trust that I am not mistaken in thinking myself disposed to go out, if I could only discover what the Lord would have me do. I must plainly confess that I have no burning desire for the conversion of the heathen, and have continually cause to lament that there is in me so little earnest desire about the salvation of souls in the district of the parish where I have hitherto been called to exercise my ministry. My reason for thinking of missionary work, and for inquiring whether or not I should personally engage in it, is the *want of labourers*. There is abundance of employment, I am fully aware, for faithful labourers at home, but this alone can be no sufficient reason for my own stay, as otherwise *all* might be at liberty to remain behind, and the heathen would not have the gospel sent to them at all.

To the Rev. W. S. Dumergue.
Church Mission House, Madras, January 12, 1847.

My dearest Walter,

From my letter to dear C. M., you will learn the arrangements made as yet about the duties I am to undertake. Bazaleel and the others whom the Lord chose to do the work of His sanctuary, He took care to endue with wisdom and understanding; I trust He will in due time act as graciously towards myself. As far as I know my own heart's intentions, I have sought to be guided to know His will as to the work I should venture to undertake. But my heart often sinks. You have little idea of the extent to which I am sometimes distressed with the feeling of my insufficiency. I am not alluding to my spiritual insufficiency now—oh that I were more conscious of it!—but to an almost entire want of several gifts which appear to be almost absolutely requisite in a person, called to act as I am or shall be, such as powers of thought, of speech, and of pen, and above all self-possession, and such self-confidence as a Christian may have, and a man ought to have. "For this," says St. Paul, "I besought the Lord thrice that it might depart from me;" and thrice, and many times thrice, have I followed his example. But it is well that I should be humbled by the continuance of my infirmity. If it be for the Lord's glory to remove the thorn, He will do it; if not, He will, I trust, not allow it to prejudice His own work and His own glory, and meanwhile will let me know and feel that His grace is sufficient for me. My dear brother, I am trying to open my heart, but have scarcely yet done so. Do pray for me. When this reaches you, I shall be looking forward, in all probability, to an almost immediate commencement of ministerial work again. Possibly, too, I may have the trials of my Cambridge Saturdays over again. However, "As thy days, so shall thy strength be."

To Miss Owen.

Dindy, April 4, 1849.

I felt much what you say, about the desire of my heart for more direct missionary work. Have you been surprised to hear no more about it? It is only occasionally that it recurs to my mind, and I am thankful to say that though I do not think my feelings are changed about it really, I am more indifferent about the nature of the work my Lord gives me to do. I think that further consideration led me to see my incompetency, as I did not at first. I bless the Lord that I do not feel the agitating the question in my mind has done me the least harm, but rather good. If there were to be some indication given me that it was His will, my desires would spring up in their former strength. But, perhaps not. I am a poor, ignorant, weak creature. How happy a thing it is to have a gracious mighty Saviour, to roll every care upon! A thought occurs to me, "Have I not been too careless of your feelings in writing about such a plan, which appears now to be a visionary one, or almost so?" What shall I say? I think you know that I would not trifle with any one's feelings, much less with those of one so highly beloved. It is a good thing for our dearest friends to manifest imperfections; it leads us more to our Friend of friends. When we see Him as He is, then we shall be able to enjoy perfect creature friends; now, it would spoil us, could we find one. I have much to thank God for in the little chillings I occasionlly meet with from dear Christian friends. I believe they were frequently creatures of my imagination. I now feel they have done me good, helping by God's grace to keep me humble. At this distance, you cannot see my imperfections as you would were I nearer, so God allows my zeal for the extension of His gospel to give you unnecessary grief.

To the Rev. David Fenn.

Kalingapatty, Night, September 23, 1858.

My dear David,

Let me assure you first of all that I never thought again of what you said in the Sattur Bungalow on the subject of selling tracts; and at the time I only thought (if I remember rightly) that I ought to be more careful in expressing myself, so as not, however unwillingly, to give pain. But if it was on your conscience, I am very, very glad you have mentioned it. I think it is very important to avoid anything that is not strictly true, either as it comes out in exaggeration, or in argument. I always fear its warping and injuring the mind; besides that, it must be grieving to the Spirit of God. And tell me, beloved brother, when I offend in this way, or in any other way. I have not written the words "tell me," without weighing their meaning, without being aware how most probably I shall shrink from the kindly counsel, and oh! perhaps, be displeased with the friend who risks my displeasure for my good. But I mean what I say; if you will only first pray to God to give me grace to bear the reproof in meekness, and to my profit; and then prepare me by telling me what you are going to do to me; and then take me aside and pray with me for the grace required. And never, if you can help it—never, at least, long—let anything I have done to displease you, remain on your mind; tell me of it. "If thy brother offend thee, tell him his fault between thee and him alone." I want—we all want—to live in peace and love. And God be praised that, much as my sins have deserved that I should forfeit the comfort of this, He has not given us over to either discord or indifference. And may we increase and abound more and more, and our love be at once out of pure hearts, and fervent; and may it not be limited to the members of our own little company! I have been more and more struck with the conclusion of your dear father's sermon, on its second reading. "'Be not many masters.' 'I have given you an example that ye should walk in My steps.' Remember you are all equally honourable and precious in His sight; let each, then, be precious and honourable in the sight of the rest."

To Miss Owen.

Sivagasi, October 21, 1858.

You are quite safe in leaving me in the hands of my gracious Saviour! But I do not think, though I cannot say that my cough is better, that there is any cause yet for anxiety. It is sometimes better, sometimes worse, and I think my strength is less; but generally I have a good appetite, and, with rare exceptions, sleep quite as well, if not better, than when I was quite free from cough. When I began again the cod liver oil, I felt a little bilious, but now I scarcely do in the least. I am anxious, and may I continue anxious, to make no mistake; to do nothing that is self-willed, or self-wise, or in the least displeasing to my blessed Master; and I humbly trust He will give me "wisdom liberally." "Good and upright is the Lord, therefore will He teach sinners in the way." "The meek will He guide in judgment." Pray for me, that He may make me meek, humble in my own eyes, and then guide me.

FREDERICK W. ROBERTSON.

XVIII.

FREDERICK W. ROBERTSON was born in 1816, was ordained in 1840, entered on his ministry at Brighton in 1847, died in 1853.

October, 1840.

With regard to my own work, I trust it is not entirely unblest, though it might well deserve to be so. We have much in this parish to encourage, and I believe the only discouragement is the sloth of my own heart, which too often produces despondency. Still, every day convinces me, more and more, that there is one thing, and but one on earth, worth living for—and that is to do God's work, and gradually grow in conformity to His image by mortification, and self-denial, and prayer. When that is accomplished, the sooner we leave this scene of weary struggle the better, so far as we are ourselves concerned. Till then, welcome battle, conflict, victory!

He writes, in 1842, on the occasion of the death of his only sister:

Dear, dear girl! you cannot dream the holiness which filled her young mind, increasing daily and rapidly, till she departed to be perfect. There had been a subdued calmness about her for years, which made the earnestness with which she sometimes expressed her opinion on vital truths more striking and more lovely. She had left us all behind, far; and when I think of her, I am disgusted with the frivolity and worldliness of my own heart. Is it credible that a man can have known Christ for six years, and believed that there is in store an inheritance whose very essence is holiness, and yet be still tampering with the seductions, follies, and passions of this wretched place? I trust this solemn scene may make us all, who have witnessed it, more earnest, and more single in heart and purpose. The days are fleeting away, and there is little done for Christ, much for self and sloth. And I sometimes shudder, when I wake, as it were, for a moment, to remember that, while we are dallying, the wheels of the chariot of the Judge do not tarry too, but are hurrying on, with what will be to some of us fearful rapidity. What need have we ever to pray for a serious, solemn mind, and an unresting sense of the presence of God within and around us! The startling silence in the room where the last of my darling sisters lies, has chilled my heart with a cold feeling of certainty that most of our life and profession is mockery. To serve the Eternal *so!*

February 26, 1849.

We do not reach spirituality of character by spasmodic unnatural efforts to crush the nature that is within us, but by slow and patient care to develope and disengage it from its evil. It is not angelic, but human excellence at which we aim, nor can we "be perfect as our Father is perfect," but in our degree, "Every man in his own order." To become saints, we must not cease to be men and women.

> "For man is not as God,
> But then most God-like, being most a man."

And if there be any part of our human nature which is essentially human, it is the craving for sympathy. The Perfect One gave sympathy, and wanted it. Gave it, as every page will show. Wanted it, "Could ye not watch with Me one hour?" "Will ye also go away?" "Simon, son of Jonas, lovest thou Me?" Found it surely, even though His brethren believed not in Him, found it in John, and Martha, and Mary, and Lazarus!

November, 1850.

I am where I was, gathering fresh accretions round the nucleus of truth; I hold surer every day that my soul and God seek each other, and am utterly fearless of the issue. I am but "an infant crying in the dark, with no language but a cry;" nevertheless, I am not afraid of the dark. It is the grand, awful mystery, but God is in it, the light of the darkest night. I am alone, lonelier than ever; . . . but the All sympathizes with me. . . . I go out into the country to *feel* God; dabble in chemistry to feel awe of Him; read the life of Christ, to understand, love, and adore Him; and my experience is closing into this, that I turn with disgust from everything to Christ. I think I get glimpses into His mind, and I am sure that I love Him more and more. A sublime feeling of a Presence comes upon me at times, which makes inward solitariness a trifle to talk about.

In 1849, after speaking of "the still country, where the heaviest laden lays down his burden at last, and has rest," he says: Yet, thank God! there is rest—many an interval of saddest, sweetest rest—even here, when it seems as if evening breezes from that other land, laden with fragrance, played upon the cheeks and lulled the heart. There are times, even on the stormy sea, when a gentle whisper breathes softly as of heaven, and sends into the soul a dream of ecstasy which can never again wholly die, even amidst the jar and whirl of waking life. How such whispers make the blood stop, and the very flesh creep, with a sense of mysterious communion! How singularly such moments are the epochs of life—the few points that stand out prominently in the recollection, after the flood of years has buried all the rest, as all the low shore disappears, leaving only a few rock-points visible at high tide!

October, 1849.

I could not quite satisfy myself with the desolate feeling which instinctively I feel as often as you talk of resolving to fix your heart on God alone. Is not this that which ought to make me supremely happy? But as I was walking in the town to-day, in a back street, and musing over this, I detected the reason of its not doing so at once. God is Life, not Death; He is not to be found, as the legion-haunted tried to find Him, among the tombs. I do think that the spirit in which you sometimes despondingly speak of living for Him alone, really means nothing more than the burial alive of a nun, who is taking the black veil, and thinking to become thus the spouse of Christ. You speak of living for God and with God, as if it were dying to all that is bright, and cheering, and beautiful, and blessed. You speak as one would speak of going into a parish union, which is good only when there is nothing else to do. No wonder that involuntarily, and without a strict analysis of the feeling, I feel a kind of shudder, and a vague cheerlessness when you talk so. No, be *vouée*, if you will; . . . but with more cheerful and grateful tones, not as if to serve God, and to hear the eternal prison doors clank behind you, were identical. Serve Him, love Him, live to Him, and you will be bright, and full of hope, and noble. "They shall renew their strength!"

1849.

A little plan, which I have found serviceable in past years, is to put down every night the engagements and duties of the next day, arranging the hours well. The advantages of this are several. You get more done than if a great part of each day is spent in contriving, and considering "what next?" A healthful feeling pervades the whole of life. There is a feeling of satisfaction at the end of the day in finding that, generally, the greater part of what is planned has been accomplished. This is the secret of giving dignity to trifles. As units, they are insignificant; they rise in importance when they become parts of a plan. Besides this—and I think the most important thing of all—there is gained a consciousness of will, the opposite of that which is the sense of impotency. The thought of Time, to me at least, is a very overpowering one—Time, rushing on, unbroken, irresistible, hurrying the worlds and the ages into being, and out of it. . . . The sense of powerlessness which this gives is very painful. But I have felt that this is neutralized by such a little plan as that. You feel that you do control your own course, you are borne on, but not resistlessly. Down the rapids you go, certainly, but you are steering and trimming your own raft, and making the flood of Time your vassal, and not your conqueror. . . . "There is nothing in the drudgery of domestic duties to soften;" you quote that. No, but a great deal to strengthen with the sense of duty done, self-control, and power. Besides, you cannot calculate how much corroding rust is *kept off*, how much of disconsolate, dull despondency is hindered. Daily use is not the jewellers' mercurial polish, but it will keep your little silver pencil from tarnishing.

1849.

I have just read Keble's hymn for the twenty-third Sunday after Trinity. The last stanza but one is truly consolatory, and those lines about the dead leaves represent a feeling which is irresistible in autumn. I recollect how sometimes the heaps of soft leaves, the fluttering of the falling ones through the air, have brought almost a pang into my heart. Do you know, sometimes they have made me think of my mother's grey hairs, with melancholy reminiscences of what she was. The unmurmuring way in which the vegetable creation resign their lives is very striking, as a thought, in connection with the great law of being, for by the sacrifice of life, voluntary or involuntary, and by that alone, can other and higher life exist. The mineral soil gives its force to the grass, and the grass its life to the cattle, and they sacrifice theirs to man; all that is involuntary, and, of course, there is nothing in it great or good. But voluntary acquiescence in, and working with, that manifested law or will of God, is the very essence of human goodness. Is it not another name for love?

November 12, 1850.

I confess the awful mystery of life, and the perplexity which hangs around the question—what it is and what it all means? Nevertheless, I am persuaded—as persuaded as I can be of anything in this world—that the meaning is good and not evil; good, I trust, to the individual as well as to the whole. There is a wondrous alchemy in time and the power of God to transmute our faults, errors, sorrows, nay, our sins themselves, into golden blessings—a truth which always appears to me prominent in the history of the Fall. The curses on man and woman, toil, etc., are all in the process of time changed into benedictions; the woman's lot itself, of subjugation and pain, becoming the very channel of her best powers of character, the condition of her devotion and her meekness. It is only the tempting devil-snake, in whose curse there is no element of alteration—only apparently a degradation, a slighter doom, no pain, but to crawl and creep and eat the dust of lower being for ever; a truth for which my whole spirit adores and blesses the ever Just. "Blessed are they that mourn, for they shall be comforted." Asked the meaning of this, surely it is plain. The tears which destroy the beauty of the outward man, channel his cheeks, cut his features with the sharp graver of anguish, are doing a glorious work on the spirit within, which is becoming fresh with all young and lively feelings.

1853.

A letter arrived from —— to-day. I did not like the expression in the one you sent me, where she speaks of the sacrifice made for ——, and the strengthening effect of sacrifice on the character. It is a bad habit of sentiment to fall into. People who make real sacrifices are never able to calculate self-complacently the good the said sacrifices are doing them; just as people who really grieve are unable at the time to philosophize about the good effects of grief. "Now no chastening for the present seemeth to be joyous, but grievous." That is true philosophy. In the lips of one struggling might and main to strengthen character, and living a life of the cross and of sacrifice, such a sentence as I have quoted might be real; as it is, it is simply unreal—a sentence got by heart, and, I think, very dangerous. Nothing is more dangerous than the command of a pen which can write correct sentiments, such as might befit a martyr or an angel. And the danger is that the confusion between a commonplace life and that of an angel or a martyr is hopeless. For when the same sublimities proceed from the lips and pens of both, who is to convince us that we are not beatified martyrs, and holy angels? Such a sentence as this would have been more real, though rather sentimental still, "How dare I talk of sacrifice? and how little of it is there in my life—one perpetual series of enjoyments!"

It has often struck me that Christ never suffered these sentimentalisms to pass without a matter-of-fact testing of what they were worth and what they meant. It is a dangerous facility of fine writing, which—I say it in deep reverence to Him—Christ would have tested by some of those apparently harsh replies which abound in His life, such as to one professing great anxiety to be with Him, saying he wished it, and not doing it, "Foxes have holes, and the birds of the air have nests, but the Son of man hath not where to lay His head."

1853.

I have found pain a humbling thing, and, what surprises me, certainly not a souring one. Many and many an hour have I spent lately incapable of even conceiving enjoyment or pleasure, and feeling as if youth and hope were settling down into premature decrepitude . . . . and yet I am grateful to say that not for years has the feeling been so true or mixed with so little bitterness, "Not as I will."

ROBERT ALFRED SUCKLING.

XIX.

ROBERT ALFRED SUCKLING was born in 1818. He entered the navy in 1831, and served till 1839. In 1840 he went to Cambridge, and was ordained in 1843. He was first of all Curate at Kennerton till 1846; and then Perpetual Curate at Bussage till his death, in 1851.

To Mrs. L——.

July 3, 1849.

I think your questions admit of all being brought under one head (Gal. v. 17), a middle point, as it were, between God and Satan—the spirit desiring to serve God, and often doing so; but as often, perhaps oftener, being conquered. This must always be the case in our conversion from the world unto God, occupying more or less time, as God in His wisdom shall see fit. It is a time full of hope, but also full of peril, for Satan will not willingly resign his share in us; it is moreover a state which *few* people get beyond. They lack the spirit of self-denial and perseverance, which ends in *always* conquering instead of *sometimes*. This, then, is what you must set before you, and aim at nothing short of it. Persevering, earnest prayer can alone, by God's grace, accomplish it; no half-measures, or efforts with halting between two opinions, but a resolute determination to be God's alone. It is evident that if God's Spirit dwelt more in us, we should always conquer. It is the gift of God's Spirit, then, which must be the special object of our prayers. Pray unceasingly for His further indwelling and guidance, and that for the sake of our Saviour, who ascended up for this very purpose to send Him down to dwell in our hearts, to be more to us than He was to His disciples, because His presence was then *external*; the Holy Spirit is in us. Be but in earnest; trifle not, but begin at once to redeem what time you can, and give it to God. I think we should find, if we dealt truly with ourselves, that the cause of all our weakness was the result of our little communion with God; our amusements, our meals, etc., these occupy our chief time, while the odds and ends, the *parings* of our time, are reserved for God. But what does He say? "Strive," and "Many will *seek*, and not be able." Set Him before you, as He alone whom you have to please, in whose presence alone joy can be found. Meditate on His love for you, pray that you may *know* the exceeding greatness of His love; then all other pleasures will seem vapid, all other desires vain. In short, you will have no other desire than to love Him, and to serve Him more and more.

To the Same.

1819.

We both grieve to hear you are not so well, and yet hope to receive better accounts from yourself. But God's will be done! and I am persuaded that you believe and feel that His will is best, whether that will be health or sickness. Such an assurance gives a peace the world knows not, cannot know, and so neither can take away, as it is touchingly expressed in Job xxxiv. 29, "When He giveth quietness, who then can make trouble?" Yet I cannot but feel this must be a sore trial for you; when God's will towards us seems determined in one direction and we have submitted to it, then for it to be changed tries us doubly. Thus, sickness seemed your lot; then came your husband's cheering account, and I had already pictured to myself the glow of health returning to your pale cheek; but to-day's account reverses it. But what then? Still His will be done, for "as thy day thy strength shall be." "He will not lay upon man more than right," and changes from health to sickness, or sickness to health, may bring us assurances nothing else can, and so may minister to us more abundant consolations; and so they will if you make them occasions of testing your own will, for such is the frailty of our nature, that unless we watch we soon begin to love God's will not for His but for its own sake; and this is proved to be so, if, when God changes His will, we cannot follow the changes without regret. So that you see all God's merciful visitations may be turned to our soul's health, and are so intended by Him; and what bystanders may deem a great trial is only to us a fresh assurance of God's loving-kindness and tender care, because we feel that whatever the trial may be, "He maketh our bed," and "giveth songs in the night," and lifteth up the soul above this narrow world to communings with Himself, the God of all consolation. Oh! those who have known the blessings of sickness can never murmur under its appointment, for then it is God makes us taste and see how gracious He is, and how blessed to trust in Him, and though He lay us low with one hand, yet with the other He holds us up, and we feel around and beneath us the everlasting arms, embracing, comforting, supporting us, cherishing us as a nurse her children. Oh! then, then it is the troubled soul returns to its rest—it has wearied itself flying up and down and seeking rest; but this world is but covered with the insatiable waters of vanity, and can give none, and so it returns to God. The pain of afflictions is but caused by ourselves. He puts forth His hand to pull us back into the ark, and we are frightened, and struggle to be free; but if we yield ourselves to His tender care, we shall find that with our ceasing to struggle comes repose and peace. His hand cannot hurt us if we rest therein. There we are safe; none can pluck us thence. All that I could say and write to you must turn on this one point, "self-resignation," having no will but God's, and if you attain that I shall beg you to be my teacher, and sit down at your feet to learn; but in proportion as we learn it we have a peace (whatever our outward trials may be) which cannot be explained, because it passeth all understanding.

To a Lady who had been his Parishioner.

1849.

I venture to write to you as a friend, to offer that consolation, which at one time would have been my duty as your pastor, in your late heavy bereavement; and yet I fear all I can say cannot reach beyond sympathy. The unerring hand of God has seen fit to remove from your visible sight one whose place none else can supply—for who can be nearer than a mother? The slight accounts which have reached us spoke of peace in her last hour, which, I trust, yet casts its shadow forth on you, forming a new bond even in death itself! She has passed through much affliction, and now all is over; never can she suffer more, never can you again weep for her earthly trials, though you may for your own loss, remembering it is her gain. And now, too, you may look back on those many trials she once suffered (and which, perhaps, perplexed you why they should be), and see God's guiding hand; how needful and necessary they were; how each cup of affliction was also full of healing medicine — a chastening of the heavenly Physician, because He loved her, and would purge away all earthly dross, that, when purified, He might take her to Himself. We cannot fail, in looking back on the afflictions of our friends, to see (though our hearts may have bled for them at the time) how needful they were. And this will teach you great lessons for the future. Tribulation is the lot, more or less, of all of us; and should they come to you—as, doubtless, many trials have, and one I know of—your mother's memory, the thought of her, the picture of her life, may rise up in dark days, to dispel the cloud, and to shed a bright light on what else were dark and mysterious. She has passed for ever from this changing world, to rest, we trust, and to join your little ——. What a strange link it is to you; on either side the dead —yet not the dead, but the living—lifting you up, bidding you leave this vain world, and fix all your thoughts on that above, where mother and child await you, perhaps watch over you and pray for you! How strange to think that a child of a few months can, and does, know what our dull senses never can; and that the one of many years has passed through a second childhood, born again, as it were, into that new kingdom! . . . I do not open a new source of grief, I trust—the thought of childhood passing pure and spotless hence cannot be such; but I would link them both together, one on either side of you, as guardian angels, to suggest pure and holy thoughts, and to speak words of peace. The one, indeed, has wrenched ties and sympathies the other never had; but why should they be broken? They need only to be purified, and we to purge our eyes of the dimness which gathers round them, as we would trace their pathway through the skies. We want but heaven to be a reality to us, a rest before us, a longed-for haven, where all our hopes are fixed, and all our affections centred; the one grand all towards which we stretch; and then we shall learn they have but ended their race first—they have reached the goal we toil for, leaving us their example to animate us on. Look back we cannot—it has nothing to attract; all lies before in the cheering end.

After the Dangerous Illness of a Child from Inflammation of the Lungs.

May 5, 1849.

Dear baby is decidedly better to-day, and begins to take a little notice of his toys again. . . . I have seen but little of sickness in children, and am perhaps more impressed with him on that account; but be that as it may, I never attended a sick-bed by the side of which I learnt so much, as I have in watching by his little cot, or at which I have witnessed so much patience. His sufferings, poor little fellow, which were extreme, were borne without a murmur. I can truly say with the poet—

> "O dearest, dearest boy, my heart
> For better love would seldom yearn,
> Could I but teach the hundredth part
> Of what from thee I learn."

Therein I saw an image of the Saviour's sufferings.

I saw them in a clearer light than I had done before, and learnt thereby how *in all things* we must become as little children before we can enter the kingdom. This little child without speech explained to me, and spoke to my heart of how He opened not His mouth and was dumb as a lamb before her shearers. For such literally was he. I can never forget his agonizing look to me for help. Mrs. Suckling's was the sterner part, and she applied the remedies. Poor child, he looked all around for help, but his eye lit only on strange faces, which increased his terror; at last he recognized me, and with a living expression of eye and face which said, "Save me!" he, by a strong effort of his weak frame, raised himself up and held out his little arms, nothing doubting I should take him; but when he saw I moved not, his features relaxed into despair, and sinking back into his mother's arms seemed to say, "Put not your trust in princes, nor in any child of man, for there is no help in them!" Instantly he seemed resigned, as if having put his trust where alone it could not be deceived. . . . I could thankfully have resigned him, had it been God's will—blessed be His name for enabling me to say so!—for there would have been the deep, all-comforting certainty of his being received into the company of those who follow the Lamb whithersoever He goeth. . . . And now life is spared I can and do with thankfulness look forward to that higher blessedness set before him, which in God's counsel is his, and I earnestly trust in His foreknowledge also, through the merits of our Redeemer. That hour of agony was caused by the alone thought that, for sin of mine, his earthly course was being shortened, and the prize of the high calling not set before him, that he might run and obtain. You may remember how, in speaking of those beautiful lines of Sewell's, I said I could not take the same view as he therein does of holy baptism, namely, that the greatest blessing he would wish for the child was to die in his baptismal holiness. I cannot look upon its blessedness as such, which when once we sin can never be attained to—as a white robe given, from which the stains of sin can never be so wholly effaced as to place the person in the same high state again. I think it a wrong way of stating the blessedness of baptism. If it were thus to be looked upon, then ought we wholly to rejoice in the death of infants, and wish them no greater blessing than to see the light and die. Such blessedness, whatever it may be, is not the blessedness of such as *do* righteousness. . . . To such a far higher blessedness belongs than the brightness of the baptismal robe, unsullied only because untried—the blessedness of such as "*overcome.*" To such, as having fought the good fight, it is said, "He that overcometh, the same shall be clothed in *white raiment,*" and to them it shall be granted "to be arrayed in fine linen, clean and white, for the fine linen is the righteousness of saints." So throughout Scripture the higher promises are to him that "overcometh."

To Miss H——.

Easter Monday, 1850.

Would I could offer you words of comfort, in the affliction which has come upon you in your dear mother's illness! She has come to a good old age, and is ripening fast, I trust, for the harvest. For herself I am persuaded she has long had such thoughts in view, and that this her illness does not surprise her; but for yourselves it is a time of deeper trial, though equally looked for. You have watched her day by day weakening, with sad hearts, yet not without bright hopes; for I am persuaded you have, with the decay of the outward man, witnessed also the renewal of the inner man. And what more could you wish? It would have been a melancholy pleasure to me to have seen her once again; but I have now no such hope. My prayers and those of my wife are with her and you; it is the one subject which engrosses our thoughts, and throws a sadness over our Easter festival. The event which we have seen in the long distance seems now near at hand; her wanderings in this wilderness are about to end, and the time of parting is sad, because the journey seems all unknown. But oh, not so, for One hath gone before who will never leave nor forsake, but will be our Guide unto death. I have often thought what a sad parting that must have been of Moses with the children of Israel in the desert; it sanctions human sorrow. He had led them as a father for forty years, and now he gathers them together to give them his parting blessing. With saddened hearts must they have beheld him turn towards the mount, with his firm step and undimmed eye, there to meet his God and die. They wept and mourned for him thirty days; but what a blessed change it was for him we catch a glimpse of on Mount Tabor! It was a sad parting; but there is yet one parting more touching, more (as the world would think) deeply bereaving; yet it is the only parting that has ever been where sorrow found no place. When our blessed Redeemer had announced His departure to His disciples, "sorrow filled their hearts," but when that most trying hour came—when He led them out as far as Bethany and blessed them, and was parted as He blessed—though they gazed up to heaven till they could see no more, yet they returned to Jerusalem *with great joy.* He was true to His word that He will never leave nor forsake; and so as their day their strength was. No bereavement was ever like that; apart from Him they would have died of grief—witness their agony during His three days' sepulture. That same power, then, my dear friends, which sustained the apostles is ready to sustain you, if you seek for it; for He has not ascended to His Father only, but to our Father as one with Him. Our griefs are His, for He knows our sorrows, and will in like manner comfort you through this sorrow. May it be a blessed season of communion with Him in suffering! is my earnest prayer; for most assuredly in affliction we feel more His presence. It is His louder voice, and the touch not only of His rod and staff, but His hand, and that hand you know was pierced for you, and as He lays it gently on you with loving look, you become more one with Him. You partake thereby of His sufferings, and learn more of His deep love in suffering for such as we; and He shares your sufferings, and then there open out to the soul, thus one with Him in suffering, thoughts, fears, hopes, joys, hitherto unknown, and we see a beauty in Him we never did before, and we wonder we ever shrank back from His healing touch, and fear lest He should ever leave us to ourselves again. My heart, indeed, bleeds for you, knowing your deep affection for your mother, and my unceasing prayer shall be, not that the sorrow be removed, but that it may be so sanctified to you, as to knit you more closely together in the mystical body of the Redeemer, and to rouse you more earnestly to trim your lamps, that when the Bridegroom comes with the company of the redeemed, you may be found watching.

To Miss ——.

March 14, 1851.

Believe me, it is a real pleasure to write to you, and, though I am rather poorly, I will endeavour to make a few remarks on your letter. "The gifts and callings of God are without repentance." No sin on our part can cancel our relationship; we are still children, He still our Father, however black our sins may be. This is the ground of confidence in approaching to Him. Esau's is no parallel case for us, but that of the Prodigal Son; was it not the ground of his confidence? This is the force of the passage in the Ephesians I pointed out, but which loses its force by the division of the verse (ch. ii. 4, 5), "God, who is rich in mercy, for His great love wherewith He loved us, *even when we were dead in sins*" (He who so loved us), "hath quickened us together with Christ." This thought runs through Isaiah, Jeremiah, especially the latter; and the great condemnation of the people was, *not* the greatness of their sins, but that when His loving mercy offered pardon they rejected it. See Isaiah i. 2, "I have nourished and brought up children, and they have rebelled against Me;" and the promise, ver. 18, "Though your sins be as scarlet, they shall be," etc. So also Jeremiah represents God as a fond parent, listening for the confession of an erring child, that He may forgive; and even when, through the stubbornness of their hearts, He is forced to punish them, He exclaims (Hosea xi. 7), "They are bent to backsliding," yet "How can I give them up?" Just as the loving parent thinks of the day when his rebellious child was just learning to speak, calls up its pretty conversations, etc., so the Almighty, ver. 3, "I taught Ephraim also to go, taking them by their arms; but they knew not that I healed them;" and again (in ch. vi. 4), "O Ephraim, what shall I do unto thee? O Judah, what shall I do unto thee?" And when justice requires that they should be punished, yet God, in punishing them, seems, as the parent, to feel more of the punishment than the child. . . . God cannot deliver a soul that loves its sin; it was not the greatness of Israel's sin that separated between them and their God, but their *cherishing* their sin— this alone separated. From all this we learn that God's face is turned from such as *love* their sins; but no shepherd's ear is so open to the bleating of his lost sheep, as the ear of Jesus is to the confession proceeding from a heart hating, or wishing or desiring to hate, its sin. It is music to His ears. Cry, then, to Him to seek and to save that which is lost; for alas! though we can walk in sin alone, yet we cannot retrace one step without His help. Look to your own helplessness, sinfulness, and confess it; but for one look at your own heart of sin, take a hundred at His face of love, *full* of mercy and compassion. . . . And recollect, we cannot love God of ourselves; our hearts can only love Him by beholding His love, and basking in its rays. . . . His love must shine down on us, and in it we must live; we can only love God as we see His love. Oh, then, beware of sin, which clouds His love! Pray with David that the heart from whence it comes may be recreated, made new, clean, written in with His law, inclined to keep it, as it is prone to transgress it. May God bless you ever, my dear child!

CHARLES KINGSLEY.

XX.

CHARLES KINGSLEY was born in 1819. He was educated at a school at Clifton, and at King's College, London. In 1838 he went up to Magdalene College, Cambridge, where he took his degree, senior opt. in mathematics and first class in classics, in 1842. He was ordained the same year to the Curacy of Eversly in Hampshire, of which place he was made rector in 1844. He was subsequently appointed one of the Queen's Chaplains in 1859; Professor of Modern History at Cambridge in 1860; Canon of Chester in 1870; Canon of Westminster in 1873. He died at Eversly in 1875.

BEFORE HIS ORDINATION.

July 7, 1842.

I have finished the first day's examination better than I expected, and though I was so nervous at first that I could hardly stand, I recovered myself tolerably afterwards. . . . I shall hope to do tolerably to-morrow, and the greater part of Saturday I shall give up to prayer and meditation and fasting.

Farnham, July 10, 1842.

God's mercies are new every morning. Here I am, waiting to be admitted in a few hours to His holy ministry, and take refuge for ever in His temple! . . . Yet it is an awful thing! for we promise, virtually at least, to renounce this day not only the devil and the flesh, but the world; to do nothing, know nothing, which shall not tend to the furtherance of God's kingdom, or the assimilation of ourselves to the Great Ideal, and to our proper place and rank in the great system whose harmony we are to labour to restore. And can we restore harmony to the Church, unless we have restored it to ourselves? If our own souls are discords to the celestial key, the immutable symphonies which revelation gives us to hear, can we restore the concord of the preplexed vibrations around us? . . . We must be holy, and to be holy we must believe rightly, as well as pray earnestly. We must bring to the well of truth a spirit purified from all previous fancies, all medicines of our own, which may adulterate the water of life! We must take of that and not of our own, and show it to mankind. It is that glory in the beauty of truth which was my idol, even when I did not practise or even know truth. And now that I know it, I can practise it and carry it out even into the details of life; now I am happy; now I am safe. . . . We need not henceforward give up the beautiful for the true, but to make the true the test of the beautiful, and the beautiful the object of the true, until to us God appears in perfect beauty! Thus every word and every leaf which has beauty in it, will be as loved as ever, but they will all be to us impulses of the divine hand, reflexes of the divine mind, lovely fragments of a once harmonious world, whose ruins we are to store up in our hearts, waiting till God restores the broken harmony, and we shall comprehend in all its details the glorious system where Christ is all in all! Thus we will love the beautiful because it is part of God, though what part it is we cannot see; and love the true because it shows us how to find the beautiful! But back, back to the thought that in a few hours my whole soul will be waiting silently for the seals of admission to God's service, of which honour I dare hardly think myself worthy, while I dare not think that God would allow me to enter on them unworthily. . . . Night and morning, for months, my prayer has been, " O God, if I am not worthy; if my sin in leading souls from Thee is still unpardoned; if I am desiring to be a deacon not wholly from the love of serving Thee; if it be necessary to show me my weakness, and the holiness of Thy office still more strongly; O God, reject me!" And while I shuddered for your sake at the idea of a repulse, I prayed to be repulsed if it were necessary, and included that in the meaning of my petition, " Thy will be done!" After this, what can I consider my acceptance but as a proof that I have not sinned too deeply for escape? as an earnest that God has heard my prayer, and will bless my ministry, and enable me not only to rise myself, but to lift others with me? O my soul, my body, my intellect, my very love, I dedicate you all to God! And not mine only . . . . to be an example and an instrument of holiness before the Lord for ever, to dwell in His courts, to purge His temple, to feed His sheep, to carry the lambs and bear them to that foster-mother, whose love never fails, whose eye never sleeps—the Bride of God, the Church of Christ.

To Lord ——.

April 25, 1852.

I am answering your letter, only just received, I fear, at a disadvantage; for first, you seem to fancy me an older man than I am. I am only two and thirty; never was a tutor of Trinity or any other college; and shall not be surprised or offended if you or any other person consider me, on further inquiry, too young to advise them. Next, I have not knowledge enough of you to give such advice as would be best for you. I have no nostrum for curing self-will and self-seeking; I am aware of none. It is a battle, I suspect a life-long battle, which each man must fight for himself, and each in his own way, and against his own private house-fiend—for in each man the evil of self-seeking takes a different form. It must do so, if you consider what it is. Self is not evil, because self is you, whom God made, and each man's self is different from his neighbour's. Now God does not make evil things, therefore He has not made self evil or wrong; but you, or self, are only wrong in proportion as you try to be something in and for yourself, and not the child of a father, the servant of a lord, the soldier of a general. So it seems to me. The fault of each man who thinks and studies as you seem to have done, in the confession with which you have honoured me, is the old fault of Lucifer. The planet is not contented with being a planet; it must be a sun; and forthwith it falls from heaven. I have no nostrum for keeping the planet in its orbit; it must keep there itself, and obey the law which was given it, and do the work which it was set to do, and then all will be well. Else it will surely find, by losing the very brightness in which it gloried, that that brightness was not its own, but a given and reflected one, which is not withdrawn from it as an arbitrary punishment for its self-seeking, but is lost by it necessarily, and *ipso facto*, when it deflects from the orbit in which alone the sun's rays can strike full upon it. You will say this is a pretty myth, or otherwise. But you have done me the honour to ask me what you are to do, and this is no answer to that question. I will try and answer as honestly as I can.

You have said boldly, in words which pleased me much, though I differ from them, that I ought not to ask you to try to cure self-seeking by idle prayer—as if a man by taking thought could add one cubit to his stature. I was pleased with the words, because they show me that you have found there is a sort of prayer which is idle prayer; and that you had sooner not pray at all than in that way. Now, of idle prayer, I think there are two kinds: one of fetish prayer, when by praying we seek to alter the will of God concerning us. This is and has been and will be common and idle enough. For if the will of Him concerning us be good, why should we alter it? if bad, what use praying to such a Being at all? Prometheus does not pray to Zeus, but curses and endures. Another is of praying to one's self to change one's self; by which I mean the common method of trying by prayer to excite one's self into a state, a frame, an experience. This, too, is common enough among Protestants and Papists, as well as among Unitarians and Rationalists. Indeed, some folks tell us that the great use of prayer is "its reflex" action on ourselves, and inform us that we can thus, by taking thought, add certain cubits to our stature. God knows the temptation to believe it is great. I feel it deeply. Nevertheless, I am not of that belief, nor, I think, are you. But if there were a third kind of prayer—the kind which is set forth to us in the Lord's Prayer, as the only one worth anything— a prayer, not that God's will concerning us or any one else may be altered, but that it may be done; that we may be kept out of all evil, and delivered from all temptation which may prevent our doing it; that we have the ἄρτον ἐπιούσιον (daily bread) given to us in body, soul, spirit, and circumstance, which will just enable us to do it and no more; that the name of Him to whom we pray may be hallowed, felt to be as noble and as sacred as it is, and acted on accordingly; and if that name were the simple name of Father, does it not seem that prayer of that kind—the prayer, not of a puling child, but of a full-grown or growing son, to his Father—a prayer to be taught duty, to be disciplined into obedience, to be given strength of will, noble purpose, carelessness of self, delight in the will and in the purpose of his Father—would be the very sort of prayer which, supposing always, as I do from ten years' experience, that Father to exist, and to hear and to love, and to have prepared good works for us to walk in—to each man his own work, and his own education for that work; does it not seem to you, I say, granting the hypothesis, that that would be a sort of prayer which would mightily help a man striving to get rid of his self-seeking, and to recover his God-appointed place in the order of the universe, and use, in that place, the attainments which his Father had given him to be used? It seems to me that such a man might look up to God, and feel himself almost strong when he was confessing his own weakness, and then look down at himself and all his learning, and see that he was most weak when he was priding himself on his own strength; that such a man would be certain to have his prayers for light, strength, unselfishness, answered, because then, indeed, his will would be working with God's will. He would be claiming to be a fellow-worker with God; to be a son going about his Father's business—in deep shame and sorrow, no doubt, for having stolen God's tools to use for his own aggrandisement for so long, but with no Papist or rather Jesuit notion of making a sacrifice to God—giving a present to Him who has already given us what we pretend to make a merit of giving Him. And such a man, it seems to me, would have no difficulty in finding out what God intended him to do; for if he really believed himself a son, under a Father's education, he would believe everything which happened to be a part of that education—every opportunity of doing good, trivial as well as grand, a duty set him by his Father to do. He would not be tempted to rush forth fanatically from the place where God had put him, to try some mighty act of self-sacrifice. If the thing which lay nearest him was the draining of a bog, or the giving employment to a pauper, or the reclaiming of a poacher, he would stay where God had put him, and try to do it, and believe that God had given him his nobility, or his learning, or his gentleman's culture, just that he might be able the better to do that part of his Father's business there and then, and no other. He would consider over what he knew, and what he could do, and would determine to make all his studies, all his self-training bear upon the peculiar position in which God had put him; not fanatically reprobating, but still considering as of less importance whatsoever did not bear on that situation. In all things, in short he would do the duty which lay nearest him, believing that *God* had put it nearest him.

And such a man, I believe, so praying, so working, keeping before him as his lode-star, "Our Father; hallowed be Thy Name; Thy kingdom come; Thy will be done on earth as it is in heaven!" and asking for his daily bread for that purpose, and no other, would find, unless I am much mistaken, selfishness and self-seeking die out of him, and active benevolence grow up in him. He would find trains of thought, and subjects of inquiry which he had pursued for his private pleasure, not to mention past sorrows and falls, turned unexpectedly to practical use for others' good; and so discover, to his delight, that his Father had been educating him while he fancied that he was educating himself. And while he was so working, and so praying, he would have neither leisure nor need to torment himself about the motives of his actions, but simply whatever his hand found to do, would do it with all his might.

To a Friend, lately Ordained, who was thinking of taking Pupils, and whom he advised to postpone the Work till he had thoroughly mastered his Parish Work.

You know, I think, why I first determined on taking pupils and employing a curate—that I might pay off money sunk by me on Church property, where I had only a life interest, to pay for the sins and neglects of my predecessors; to enable me to give up a sinecure, hateful and burdensome to my conscience; to enable me to build and organise schools, and other social improvements in the parish, as opportunity offered. I hoped also that the work of pupils would be a healthy training for my own mind on points necessarily long neglected; that it might give me an opportunity of saving a young heart or two from this untoward generation. . . . That by leaving the parish routine work in the hands of a devoted and methodical man, I might find time to labour on those social questions to which I cannot but believe myself by strange providences, specially called. I may have been mistaken, God knows, "the heart is deceitful above all things!" I may have mistaken laziness and ambition for the voice of God. . . . I may have incurred the prophet's rebuke, "Thou hast kept other vineyards, but thine own vineyard hast thou not kept." And you may have a perfect right to ask me why I should press upon you an entire devotion of your time to priestly labour, which I did not impose on myself? But I may answer that I bought this cessation by seven years of weary, single-handed, up-hill toil, ending in a severe illness from over-exertion; that I ate my bread in heaviness of heart for very labour and anxiety, let me have seemed as cheerful as I may; and found optics and Homer real relaxations from the crushing weight of an enormous nightmare object, which seemed vaster and more difficult the more I toiled to master it. No wonder, then, if I was tempted to ask some one else to take the simpler (though not less holy or less awful, or requiring less utter devotion, self-restraint, methodic exertion) functions of my calling off my hands for a while—perhaps in the conceited hope of indoctrinating him with my own ideas, and stirring him up to outstrip me—which may God grant—in the great work of uniting the Catholic Church of the past with the inevitable democracy of the future.

For such an object, and just as much for the work of preaching Christ's gospel to the poor, awakening the souls of old women, and telling little children of their Father in heaven, there is needed continual self-examination, self-restraint, continual pains to bring every talent to bear on God's work, to develope and train, even by the most mechanical drudgery, every faculty one finds in one's self. One must give Christ all, and the very best which we can make of all, for it is His already, bought with His own blood. You may thank God if you have been spared those hours of bitter agony and remorse, those humbling and heart-searching sins, which drive men to Christ like cured demoniacs, to cling desperately to His feet, and refuse to stir from them again for ever; but surely you will be the last to make the absence of those fearful experiences an excuse for less intense loyalty to Him who has preserved you from them. That you would never do so consciously, I well know (but we do many things in practice, which we should shudder at in reflection); and ask yourself whether your as yet sunny and simple life, to which melancholy itself is a sort of graceful and luxurious phase, may not be keeping you sporting somewhat too much on the surface of things, keeping you from those awful questions, more awful than any metaphysical or dialectic speculations in the world—is my heart right with God? Do I know that wheresoever my will is not utterly His will, I am a sinner and a rebel? How shall I do His work before the night cometh wherein no man can work? How shall I be faithful in a few things, that He may make me ruler over many things? Am I wrapped up in systems and formulæ, even when I am declaiming against them, or am I looking face to face at Almighty God Himself, and the spiritual world of sin and righteousness, heaven and hell on earth? These questions may seem harsh and impertinent; but, my dear friend, I warn you, in the name of God, that the day is fast coming when no man can work, but only take his wages, such as they are. We live in a time more awful than the world has seen since the Reformation—more awful even than that. The day of the Lord is at hand. Then every man whose heart is not whole with God must be content to have the whole foundations of his faith battered, ground to powder, stone by stone, go down into the hell of doubt, disbelief, perhaps sheer Atheism or Popery, which is in some cases but Atheism in purple and fine linen. Affliction, persecution, calumny, will be the lot of every man who dares preach the kingdom of God, and the living Church of the living Christ. Then every man's work will be tried with fire, be sifted with the sieve of vanity, and tried in the fire of the wrath of God. . . . God give you grace to stand in that day; I may fall for aught I know; I should fall now daily, and give up God as a hard taskmaster, and Christ as a bygone legend, did I not hope and trust utterly that He who has brought me thus far will never leave me nor forsake me, will drive me back with the thunderbolts of His wrath every time I dare wander or grow lazy. Oh, my dear friend, pray for me and for yourself, that we may never need those thunderbolts—never need to be taught by bitter shame and agony, how little we have really loved, served, trusted Him of whom we talked so glibly!

To Miss ——, on the Death of her Mother.

Chester, May, 1871.

We were much shocked at the news, and all felt deeply for you.

And now what shall I say? I am not going to tell you impertinent commonplaces as to how to bear sorrow. I believe that the wisest plan is sometimes not to try to bear it—as long as one is not crippled for one's everyday duties—but to give way to sorrow utterly and freely. Perhaps sorrow is sent that we *may* give way to it, and in drinking the cup to the dregs, find some medicine in it itself, which we should not find if we began doctoring ourselves, or letting others doctor us. If we say simply, "I am wretched; I ought to be wretched;" then we shall perhaps hear a voice, "Who made thee wretched but God? Then what can He mean but thy good?" And if the heart answers impatiently, "My good? I don't want it, I want my love;" perhaps the voice may answer, "Then thou shalt have both in time."

HEDLEY VICARS.

XXI.

HEDLEY VICARS was born in 1826, and obtained his commission in the army in 1843. He first began to think seriously in 1848. In 1854 he was ordered with his regiment to the Crimea, and fell mortally wounded in a night attack of the Russians before Sebastopol, on March 22, 1855.

To a Friend.

1851.

As my last hurried note was indeed but a poor apology for a letter, I must write a few lines to-day. "They that feared the Lord spake often one to another," and what time more fitting and appropriate in which to express the thoughts of our hearts towards Jesus, than just after the sweet and refreshing enjoyments of His day? For when is the fragrant dew of His Holy Spirit poured so largely on our souls, as on those days of heaven upon earth? I remember, alas! too well the time when I dreaded the return of Sunday, and considered it both dull and tedious, but now surely no day is so cheering and delightful, and there is none that passes away so quickly. I recollect that, for several months, the only inward sanctifying proof I could, on examination, bring to assure myself that I had indeed been made an heir of Christ, was this longing desire for the Lord's day. . . . I had a delightful conversation, a few days ago, with a young corporal who left my company a short time since. He has been for nearly three years a consistent follower of Christ, and I am proud to say he is still fighting the good fight of faith. But we must expect to have the bitter as well as the sweet. I grieve to say that one, of whom I had great hopes, has deserted his colours, and gone back. Poor fellow! I deeply pity him. I trust it may prove a warning lesson to me, to watch and pray more constantly and fervently, and "take heed," lest I also fall. But I will never give up any man—Jesus did not give *me* up—and I hope and look to his being brought back to the fold. What you said in your letter about spiritual pride, I feel to be very applicable to myself at times, but when I am so inclined to forget who and what I am, I endeavour to imagine the sinner standing alone, without a Saviour, and without the Holy Ghost; and the miserable wretched thought quickly makes me to know and feel my utter vileness and weakness!

To the Same.

1854.

I thank you very much for your valued letter, which affected me not a little. We are, as far as men can judge, on the eve of war; and I shall soon, perhaps, be engaged in all the horrors of battle. But even then, believe me, I shall ever remember with deepest gratitude the friend who has so often cheered and comforted my too cold and wavering heart. But there are some things in your letter which grieve me. Your heart is sorrowful. I have felt more than once that peculiar bitterness which your soul has so lately experienced, and I can, therefore, fully sympathize with you. When we have, as we fondly hoped, been blessed by God in bringing a fellow-sinner into the fold of Christ, and when that often-prayed-for and yearned-over one has given many proofs which, both to ourselves and to the world in which he moves, appear decisive, it goes to the heart's quick to see or hear of such turning his back on an ever-loving and ever-suffering Saviour, and going once more hand in hand with His bitterest enemy. It is not so much, perhaps, fear for the souls of those poor erring men which causes us that sickness and weariness of heart; for we know that when a man sins, he "has an Advocate with the Father, even Jesus Christ the righteous;" and do you not think that in praying for the backslider we seem to see the day of his repentance near again? But what tongue can tell the injury that is done to the cause of Christ? And this, alas! is irrevocable. But, dear friend, let us not dwell on this painful subject. Each returning day proclaims loudly in our ears, "Now is the accepted time! now is the day of salvation!" bidding us *never* despair, for while there is breath there is hope; but rather calling us to lay out ourselves afresh, and begin the battle again. I feel for you very much, and still more for poor W—— and H——, who have been at length overcome by the all-enticing snares of Satan. (Oh how long he had me completely in his net!) The temptations, in the wild roving life those poor fellows lead, must be strong. But we will unite our prayers for their recovery, and hope and believe (as I do still in the similar case of two or three of my soldiers) they will be attracted again to the cross of Jesus. We may conclude that, when a soul has indeed tasted of its sweet comfort, the pleasures which once satisfied lose their charm, and appear but empty shadows, and, therefore, that it will find no rest until it returns to the sinner's refuge. When I hear of and see others wandering from the Good Shepherd, I cannot help thinking to myself, "And who art *thou*, that thou shouldst be preserved?" Surely there is no safety but in Jesus, in clinging to His cross. I followed a poor sergeant to his last home yesterday, and now the mournful notes of the "Dead March" proclaim that another soldier is being carried to the same resting-place. These sudden deaths are warnings to us to be likewise ready. We are still very unsettled—nothing being known for certain as to our movements. When it is known I will tell you. I have just heard from my beloved mother. She tells me she has a letter from you, full of sympathy and comfort, and that she trusts a friendship is now established between both families which will last for ever. God for ever bless you for comforting her!

March 31.

I have left the quiet peace and heavenly calm of blessed Beckenham, soon, perhaps, to enter upon scenes of angry warfare and strife; but be assured, dearest friends, that you will ever live in my memory, my thoughts, and my prayers; and should it be God's will that we should not see each other here again, we will not sorrow even as others which have no hope, for if we believe (which, thank God, we do!) that Jesus died and rose again, even so them also that sleep in Jesus will God bring with Him. Death to the believer is, after all, only an incident in immortality, for Christ says, "He that believeth on Me *hath* everlasting life." How earnestly I thank my heavenly Father for having led me betimes to prepare for that certain eternity beyond the grave! A soldier needs to have Christ in his heart before the hour of battle, though we may hope and believe that to many (like the dying thief) "the Sun of Righteousness may arise with healing in His wings," even after the swift bullet has brought the awful message, "Behold, this night (or this hour) thy soul shall be required of thee!" I had such a heavenly joy yesterday and to-day, in conversing with a young bandsman and a corporal, whom I sent for to my room. I was much struck by an observation from the latter (who for a time had fallen away, but is now all right), "I want more of Jesus in this life, sir, so that when I die I may not be admitted into heaven as a stranger, but be received like a long-lost child would be at his own home." Surely the Spirit of God is at work in his soul. These two men began their Christian course at the same time as myself. I experience fresh delight every time I speak with them of the love of God, of the peace and joy there is in believing. Alas! we understand each other, too, when we speak of our weakness, our deadness at times to spiritual perceptions, our cares, our temptations. The Testaments for the men arrived safely. Poor fellows! they were so delighted to get them. I greatly like the soldier's prayer. Short, strong, and easy to be understood, it comprehends all that will fit us for heaven. Being a soldier, I take the liberty to use it myself. God grant they may all offer it from the ground of the heart! I have often heard it said, "The worse the man, the better the soldier." Facts contradict this untruth. Were I ever, as leader of a forlorn hope, allowed to select my men, it would be most certainly from among the soldiers of Christ, for who should fight so fearlessly and bravely as those to whom death presents no after terrors?

I cannot tell you how lonely I always feel, when, after having enjoyed your society, I have once more returned to the routine of a soldier's life. But do not suppose because I say this, or from anything I have lately said, that I am beginning to show the white feather, and that, finding a soldier's cross too irksome, I would change it for one less weighty. *Never!* The Lord has called me to eternal life in the army, and as a soldier I will die. Had I loved Jesus when I was seventeen, or rather, had the love of Jesus been then made known to my soul, I certainly should not have been a soldier; but as it is, death alone shall make me leave my colours. Did our God and King, Jesus Himself, the great "Captain of our salvation," spare no toil, fatigue, anguish, or bodily suffering even unto death, to obtain forgiveness of our sins? and shall not we, towards whom this infinite love and compassion have been shown, be constrained to do something for Jesus in return, nor care if our path of duty should prove a rough and thorny one—for He cleared a way through the briars first, and we but follow in the Saviour's footsteps? I confess that at times Satan has puffed me up, and made me think more highly of myself than I ought to think; but I hate and detest this sin, and for many months I think the Lord has given me grace to fight against it effectually. But I must be watchful. . . . I often grieve when at night I look back on the many precious hours of the day lost, given me for the purpose of making a closer acquaintance with Jesus; and I suppose the greater happiness we find in Him here, the greater will be our enjoyment of Him hereafter. It is only adding sorrow to grief to know as we do that Christ yearns for our love, and that it pains His human nature when forgotten by us, for whom He has done such great things; but I do desire to be always in Christ, and He in me; and I think in His mercy God is leading my heart to seek more earnestly the "unsearchable riches of Christ;" and yet there is still the remains of the old leaven working in my heart, and it is only the grace of God that restrains me. But how comforting the assurance that He will carry on the labour of love in our souls, that He does not leave the issue the least doubtful! for His having come to us and made His abode with us, filling our hearts with peace and joy in believing, and causing them to "abound with hope through the power of the Holy Ghost," is a proof that we shall persevere unto the end, and leads us to believe that (notwithstanding our frail nature) we shall never perish, but, being sealed with the Spirit of promise, be kept through faith unto salvation, and preserved blameless unto the coming of our Lord Jesus Christ.

To Miss Vicars.

Piræus, September 27-30, 1854.

It is a very gloomy day, the sky black and lowering, and the rain descending in torrents. I was meditating just now on this bleak scene of dreary solitude—my only companion a little quail—and thinking over the strange and often appalling sights my eyes have looked upon, in the realities of death and the grave, since God called me here. As these ideas floated through my mind, the train of thought suddenly changed, and the dismal view without, and the cold and dreary room I occupy, brought before me the "Man of Sorrows"—Jesus—who once weathered the stormy tempest for you and me, and of whom it may be said, from the manger to the grave, that He had not where to lay His head. It is so soothing to the soul, in seasons of cloud and distress, to know that Jesus hath borne our griefs and carried our sorrows, and to rest on the tender kindness of Him who has said, "As one whom his mother comforteth, so will I comfort you." . . . Oh, dearest Mary, it is well to have the love of Jesus Christ in its reality in our hearts! What solid peace and rich enjoyment we obtain by looking unto Jesus! Where else shall we behold the boundless love of our heavenly Father? What else could have led me to the side of men dying of pestilence? for how could I have spoken to these men of the love of God without looking to Jesus? And to whom could I implore them to look but to Jesus? . . . I have witnessed the effect of even the name of Jesus; I have noticed a calm and peaceful look pass more than once over the ghastly face of the dying as that blessed name passed my lips. . . . I do not think I ever told you of Craney's happy death. Shortly before he breathed his last he asked Dr. Twining to read Romans viii. to him. As he read, the dying man's breath became shorter and shorter and his face brighter; and as the last words fell upon his ear, "Nor height, nor depth, nor any other creature, shall be able to separate us from the love of God, which is in Christ Jesus our Lord," he said, "Thank you, sir; that will do," and died.

October 18.

I have but just emerged from clouds, which have obscured Jesus from my view. I seemed to wander in thick darkness, without my loving Redeemer near me to be my stay and delight. But great blessings are often sent to us after short trials; and such, I think, I am now finding. The Lord Jesus has arisen upon me, and has made His glory manifest to my soul. I feel less *tied down* to this world than I did, and more ready to depart and be with Christ! Sometimes I long to do so, from fears, lest I should ever (I do not say, fall away, but) do anything which would dishonour my Saviour. And yet what is this but cowardice—wishing to leave the battle-strife of earth for the repose of heaven, with Jesus? Oh! rather would I wait patiently, and look for the coming of the Lord. Shall we not hail that bright and glorious day? . . . I knew you would enter into my disappointment in not having been ordered on to the Crimea ere this. To say I have not felt it (yes, and deeply, too!), would be saying what is not true. But I hope I can leave it in the hands of my God and Saviour, sure that He orders everything for the best. . . . Decision and courage at first are absolutely necessary for an officer who wishes to become a soldier of the cross. Without such he will have endless difficulties and trials, and will have no peace given him by those who oppose, until he returns to the allegiance of the god of this world, or else *fearlessly shows his colours.*

Piræus, November 2, 1854.

We are all busily preparing for active service, so I have not much time to spare; but as there may not be another opportunity, I hasten to write a few farewell lines. There are times when the heart feels more powerfully drawn to those whom it loves best. It is so with me now. . . . Before this letter reaches its destination, we shall probably be in front of the enemy. God alone knows whether we shall ever meet again in this world; but after all, what are the few short years we might have lived in the enjoyment of each other's friendship here, compared to that endless eternity we shall spend together beyond the grave? My soul has lately had to weather many a stormy billow, but I feel quite peaceful and happy now; my own strength was feeble to resist, but Jesus has conquered Satan, and never did I love that blessed Saviour more than I do on this day. . . . Yesterday I was on guard. About twelve o'clock at night, whilst reading 2 Cor. v., I had such inward joy and peace and comfort, that I felt strongly inclined to waken the poor fellows who were stretched asleep on the guard bed in the adjoining room, to pray with them and to talk to them of the love of Christ! And thus it is (for it seems so selfish to keep all this happiness pent up in one's own heart, when it might be shared by others), whenever I have been brought nearest to my Saviour. . . . I have been constrained and forced, while the fire burns, to speak with my tongue, and to make use of the golden hours of communion with Jesus in the solitude of my chamber, to publish what the Lord Jesus has done for my soul—even for me, than whom a man more undeserving His mercy does not exist. I felt so happy and merry in that miserable guard-room yesterday. I always make it a rule, after reading to the men the "orders of the guard," to warn them against the too prevalent habit of swearing, and, to my great delight, during my whole tour of duty, I did not hear one oath; and in addition to this, I had the pleasure of hearing several times the rustling of the leaves of the tracts I had given them, and two or three times, as I passed through the rooms, I could see them poring over them. . . . It grieves me to think of the sorrow it will cause to my L—— and to you, should anything happen to me; but for myself I fear not. If I were trusting in myself in any way, I might indeed tremble at the whistling of every bullet, and dread being summoned in an instant before the judgment seat of Christ; but I can see no cause for alarm, even at the very moment when soul and body are about to separate, with the crimson cross in full view.

To his Mother.

Camp before Sebastopol, February 19, 1855.

As I gazed on this magnificent scenery, on the wildness and grandeur of the lofty, snow-capped mountains, giving an additional charm to the surrounding loveliness, all around was so still and calm that my thoughts wandered to more peaceful climes, and to that not far distant day, when Jesus shall return to His beautiful, although sin-marred world, when wars shall cease for ever, and love and holiness fill the breasts of His redeemed people. Oh, dearest mother, there are times when I long for this final consummation of all things! What a blessed thing it will be to serve Christ, with a heart wholly renewed and made like unto His; when sin can no more afflict us with its presence, or bow us down under its intolerable burden! But it is not always thus that my soul longs and pants for that great advent of my glorious and precious Saviour. Oh that I were *ever* waiting and ready to welcome Him, on His triumphant return to a world, where once "He took upon Him the form of a servant," to redeem and save sinners! May He give me grace to bear His cross, and to follow Him daily, be the way smooth or rough! I have often reason to grieve that my love for my Saviour is so small. But then His love "passeth knowledge," and in looking unto Him and taking refuge in His cross, I find sure safety, rest, and peace.

February 28.

Oh that the Lord God would come amongst us with a "high hand and with a stretched-out arm"! that He would by the mighty power of the Holy Spirit change and soften the hard hearts of those who despise the riches of His grace, and who make a mock at sin, whilst standing upon the verge of eternity! ... I cannot but believe that many have died in peace and hope, for I have heard from the lips of several, in their dying hours, that their only hope was through the mercy of Him who died on the cross. But it grieves me when I look around, and see how few, how very few, there are amongst the yet strong and healthy (who may in a moment be numbered with the dead) who show any love for Jesus; but it is only through sovereign grace that *we* have beheld the Lamb crucified *for us*, and have been brought to rejoice in Him, who purchased us with His own blood, with "joy unspeakable and full of glory." Knowing, as I do, the sin-stained course of my past life, and how utterly undeserving I was of being an object of God's mercy, I never despair of even the foremost in the ranks of Satan being brought to the feet of Jesus; and when I see one, for whose conversion I have prayed, becoming more hardened in sin, I comfort myself with the thought that grace led *my* roving feet to tread the heavenly road, and the same constraining power may, at any moment, convince him of sin, and reveal Jesus to his soul.

Written Twenty-four Hours before his Death.

The greater part of another month is past, and here I am still kept by the protecting arm of the Almighty from all harm. I have been in many a danger by night and by day since I last wrote to you; but the Lord has delivered me from them all, and not only so, but He has likewise kept me in perfect peace, and made me glad with the light of His countenance. In Jesus I find all I want of happiness and enjoyment, and as week after week and month after month roll by, I believe He is becoming more and more lovely in my eyes, and precious to my soul.

JOHN COLERIDGE PATTESON.

XXII.

JOHN COLERIDGE PATTESON, son of Mr. Justice PATTESON, was born in 1827, ordained deacon in 1853, sailed for New Zealand 1855, consecrated bishop 1861, was martyred by the natives of the island Nukapu 1871.

To Mrs. Martin, after Settling to go out with the Bishop of New Zealand.

1854.

I pray God that I may have chosen aright, and that if I have acted from sudden impulse too much, from love of display, or from desire to raise some interest about myself, or from any other selfish and unholy motive, it may be mercifully forgiven. Now at all events I must pray that with a single honest desire for God's glory I may look straight onwards towards the mark. I must forget what is behind, I must not lose time in analysing my state of mind to see how, during years past, this wish has worked itself out. I trust the wish is from God, and now I must forget myself, and think only of the work whereunto I am called. But it is hard to flesh and blood to think of the pain that I am causing my dear, dear father and the pain I am causing others outside my own circle here. But they are all satisfied that I am doing what is right.

To his Sister.

Auckland, July 11, 1855.

I do not doubt that I am where I ought to be. I do think and trust that God has given me this work to do; but I need earnest prayers for strength that I may do it. It is no light work to be suddenly transplanted from a quiet little country district to a work exceeding in magnitude anything that falls to the lot of an ordinary parish priest in England—in a strange land, among a strange race of men, in a newly forming and worldly society. It is well that I am hearty and sound in health, or I should be regularly overwhelmed with it. Two texts I think of constantly, "Whatsoever thy hand findeth to do, do it with all thy might;" "Sufficient for the day," etc. I hardly dare look forward to what my work may be on earth; I cannot see my way; but I feel sure that He is ordering it all, and I try to look on beyond the earth, when at length, by God's mercy, we may all find rest.

That I have been so well in body and cheerful in mind ever since I left home—I mean cheerful on the whole, not without seasons of sadness, but so mercifully strengthened at times—must, I think, without any foolish enthusiasm, be remembered by me as a special act of God's goodness and mercy. I was not the least weary of the sea. . . . But what most surprises me is this; that when I am alone, as here at night in a great, cheerless, lonely room, as I should have thought it once, though I can't help thinking of my own comforts at home, and all dear faces around me, though I feel my whole heart swelling with love to you all, still I am not at all sad and gloomy, or cast down. This does surprise me. I did not think it would or could be so. I have, indeed, prayed for it, but I had not faith to believe that my prayer would be so granted. . . . It may be otherwise, any day, of course ; and to what else can I attribute this fact, in all soberness of mind, but to the mercy of God strengthening me for my work?

To the Same.

September 11, 1855.

Sometimes I cannot help wishing that I could say all this, but not often. There is One who understands, and in really great trials even, it is well to lean only on Him. But I must write freely. You will not think me moody and downhearted, because I show you that I do miss you, and often feel lonely and shut up in myself. This is exactly what I experience, and I think that if I were ill, as you often are, I should break down under it, but God is very merciful to me in keeping me in very good health. . . . I never, perhaps, shall know fully how it is, but somehow, as a matter of fact, I am on the whole cheerful, and always busy, and calm in mind. I don't have tumultuous bursts of feeling, and overwhelming floods of recollection, that sweep right away all composure. Your first letters upset me more than once as I re-read them, but I think of you all habitually with real joy and peace of mind. . . . Yet in the midst of all I half doubt sometimes whether everything about and within me is real—I just move on like a man in a dream; but this again does not make me idle. I don't suppose I ever worked harder on the whole than I do now, and I have much anxious work at the hospital.

To his Father.

1860.

My dear Father,
        You can hardly tell how difficult I find it to be, amidst all the multiplicity of works, a man of devotional, prayerful habits; how I find from time to time that I wake up to the fact, that while I am doing more than I was in old times, yet that I pray less. How often I think that "God gives" to the bishop "all that sail with him," that the work is prospering in his hands; will it prosper in mine? I know He can use any instrument to His glory. I know that, and that He will not let my sins and shortcomings hinder His projects of love and blessing to these Melanesian Islanders; but as far as purity of motive, and a spirit of prayer and self-denial go for anything in making up the qualification on the human side for such an office—in so far, do they exist in me? You will say I am over-sensitive, and expect too much. That I think very likely may be true. It is useless to wait till one becomes really fit, for that of course I shall never

be. But while I believe most entirely that grace does now supply all our deficiencies when we seek it fully, I do feel frightened when I see that I do not become more prayerful, more real in communion with God. This is what I must pray for earnestly. . . . You all think that absence from relations, living upon yams, want of the same kind of meat and drink that I had at home—that these things are proofs of sincerity. I believe that they all mean just nothing when the practical result does not come to this—that a man is walking more closely with his God.

To the Same, a few Days before his Consecration as Bishop.

1861.

I ought not to shrink back now. The thought has become familiar to me, and I have the greatest confidence in the judgment of the Bishop of New Zealand; and I need not say how your words and letters and prayers are helping me now. Indeed, though at any great crisis of our lives, no doubt, we are intended to use more than ordinary strictness in examining our motives, and in seeking for greater grace, deeper repentance, more earnest and entire devotion to God, and amendment of life, yet I know that any strong emotion, if it existed now, would pass away soon, and that I must be the same man as bishop as I am now, in this sense, that I shall have just the same faults, unless I pray for strength to destroy them, and that all my characteristic and peculiar habits of mind will remain unchanged by what will only change my office and not myself. So that where I am indolent now I shall be indolent henceforth, unless I seek to get rid of indolence; and I shall not be at all better, or wiser, or more consistent as a bishop, than I am now, by reason simply of being a bishop. You know my meaning. Now I apply what I write to prove that any strong excitement now would be no proof of a healthy state of mind. . . . You know, my dearest father, that I do not undervalue the grace of ordination; only I mean that the right use of any great event in one's life, as I take it, is not to concentrate *feeling* so much on it, as earnestness of purpose, prayer for grace, and for increase of simplicity and honesty and purity of heart. Perhaps other matters affect me more than my supposed state of feeling, so that my present calmness may be attributed to circumstances of which I am partially ignorant; and, indeed, I do wonder that I am calm, when one moment's look at the map, or thought of the countless islands, almost overwhelms me. How to get at them? Where to begin? How to find men and means? How to decide upon the best mode of teaching? But I must try to be patient, and to be content with very small beginnings, and endings, too, perhaps.

Again, on Sunday Night, after his Consecration.

The bishop spoke of you in his sermon with faltering voice, and I broke down; yet at the moment of the "Veni Creator" being sung over me, and the imposition of hands, I was very calm. The Bible presented is the same you gave me, with your love and blessing, on my fifth birthday. Oh, my dear, dear father, God will bless you for all your love to me, and your love to Him in giving me to His service. May His heavenly blessing be with you and all your dear ones for ever!

To the Same.

April 29, 1861.

What some of you say about self-possession on one's going about among the people being marvellous, is just what of course appears to me commonplace. Of course it is wrong to risk one's life, but to carry one's life in one's hand is what other soldiers besides those of the cross do habitually, and no one, as I think, would willingly hurt a hair of my head in Melanesia, or that part of it where I am at all known. How I think of those islands! How I see those bright coral and sandy beaches, strips of burning sunshine fringing the masses of forest rising into ridges of hills, covered with a dense mat of vegetation! Hundreds of people are crowding on them, naked, armed, with wild uncouth cries and gestures. I cannot talk to them but by signs. But they are my children now. May God enable me to do my duty by them! I have now as I write a deepening sense of what the change must be that has passed over me. Again I go, by God's blessing, for seven months to Melanesia. But what may be the result? Who can tell? You know it is not of myself that I am thinking. If God of His great mercy lead me in His way, to me there is little worth living for but the going onward with His blessed work.

Two short extracts from letters of Sir JOHN PATTESON are here introduced.

April, 1861.

MY OWN DEAREST COLEY,

How many more letters you may receive from me, God only knows, but, as I think, not many. The iodine fails altogether, and has produced no effect on the swellings in my throat; on the contrary, they steadily increase, though not rapidly. Doubtless they will have their own course, and, in some way or other, deliver my soul from the burden of the flesh. Oh may it by God's mercy be the soul of a faithful man! Faith and love I think I have, and have long had; but I am not so sure that I have really repented of my past sins, or only abandoned them when circumstances had removed, almost, the temptation to commit them. Yet I do trust that my repentance has generally been sincere, and though I may have fallen again, that I may by God's grace have also risen again. I have no assurance that I have fought the good fight, like St. Paul, and that henceforth there is laid up a crown of gold; yet I have a full and firm hope that I am not beyond the pale of God's mercy, and that I may have hold of the righteousness of Christ, and may be partaker of that happiness which He has purchased for His own by His atoning blood. No other hope have I; and, in all humility, I from my heart feel that any apparent good I may have done has been His work in me, and not my own. May it please Him that you and I, my dear son, may meet hereafter, together with all those blessed ones, who have already departed this life in His faith and fear, in His kingdom above!

June 12, 1861.

Oh, my dearest, right reverend, well beloved son, how I thank God that it has pleased Him to save my life until I heard of the actual fact of your being ordained and consecrated, as I have said more than once since I heard of it! May it please Him to prolong your life very many years, and to enable you to fulfil all those purposes for which you have now been consecrated, and that you may see the fruit of your labour of love before He calls you to heaven! But if not, may you have laid such foundations for the spread of God's Word throughout the countries committed to your charge, that when it pleases God to summon you hence, you may have a perfect consciousness of having devoted all your time and labour, and, so far as you are concerned, have advanced all the works as fast and as serenely as it seemed fit to your great Assister, the Holy Spirit, that they should be advanced! Only conceive that an old judge of seventy-two, cast out of his own work by infirmity, should yet live to have a son in the holy office of bishop, all men rejoicing round him! and so, indeed, they do rejoice around me, mingling their loving expressions at my illness and approaching death.

LETTER FROM BISHOP PATTESON TO HIS FATHER.

1861.

It may be that, as I write, your blessed spirit, at rest in paradise, may know me more truly than ever you did on earth; and yet the sorrow of knowing how bitter it is within may never be permitted to ruffle your everlasting peace. I may never see you on earth. All thought of such joy is gone. I did really cling to it (I see it now) when most I thought I was quite content to wait for the hope of the great meeting. I will remember and endeavour to do what you said about all business matters.

I will pray God to make me more desirous and more able to follow the holy example you leave behind. Oh that the peace of God may be given to me also when I come to die! though how may I dare to hope for such an end, so full of faith and love and the patient waiting for Christ?

I must go on with my work. I must try to turn to good account among the islands this great opportunity. Oh how much more sorrow and heavy weight on my heart! I am quite worn out and weary. It seems as if the light were taken from me, as if it were not longer possible to work away so cheerily when I have no longer you to write to about it all, no longer your approval to seek, your notice to obtain.

I must go on writing to you, my own dearest father, even as I go on praying for you. It is a great comfort to me, though I feel that, in all human probability, you are to be thought of now as one of the blessed drawn wholly within the vail. Oh that we may all dwell together hereafter, for His blessed sake who died for us! Now, more than ever, your loving, dutiful son.

To his Sister, on the Loss of one of his Young Native Converts, who had been Wounded by a Poisoned Arrow.

We buried him at sea. . . . Patience and trust in God, the same belief in His goodness and love, that He orders all things for our good, that this is but a proof of His merciful dealings with us: such comforts God has graciously not withheld. I never felt so utterly broken down, when I thought and think of the earthly side of it all; never, perhaps, so much realized the comfort and power of His presence, when I have had grace to dwell upon the heavenly and abiding side of it. I *do*, with my better part, heartily and humbly thank Him, that He has so early taken these dear ones to their own everlasting home. I think of them, with blessed saints, our own dear ones in paradise, and, in the midst of my tears, I bless and praise God. But, dear Fan, Fisher most of all supplied to me the absence of earthly relations and friends. He was my boy: I loved him as, I think, I never loved any one else. I don't mean *more* than you all, but in *a different way*; not as one loves another of equal age, but as a parent loves a child. I can hardly think of my little room at Kohimarama without him. I long for the sight of his dear face, the sound of his voice. It was my delight to teach him, and he was clever and so thoughtful and industrious. I know it is good that my affections should be weaned from all things earthly. I try to be thankful, and I think I am thankful really; time will do much, God's grace much more. I only wonder how I have borne it all. "In the multitude of the sorrows that I had in my heart, Thy comforts have refreshed my soul." . . . However much I may reproach myself with want of caution, and of prayer for guidance (and this is a bitter thought), they were in the simple discharge of their duty. Their intention and wish were to aid in bringing these poor people to the gospel of Christ. It has pleased God that in the execution of this great purpose they should have met with their deaths. . . . This letter was begun on your birthday. It has been written with a heavy dull weight of sorrow on my heart, yet not unrelieved by the blessed consciousness of being drawn, as I humbly trust, nearer to our most merciful Father in heaven, if only by the very impossibility of finding help elsewhere. It has not been a time without its own peculiar happiness. How much of the Bible seemed endued with new powers of comfort! . . . How true it is that they who seek find! "I sought the Lord and He heard me." The closing chapters of the gospels, 2 Corinthians, and how many other parts of the New Testament were blessings indeed! Jeremy Taylor's "Life of Christ," and "Holy Living and Dying," "Thomas à Kempis," most of all, of course, the Prayer-book, and such solemn memories of our dear parents and uncles, such blessed hopes of reunion, death brought so near, the longing (*if only not unprepared*) for the life to come; I could not be unhappy. Yet I could not sustain such a frame of mind long. . . . But, thanks be to God, it is not altogether an unhealthy sorrow, and I can rest in the full assurance that all this is working out God's purposes of love and mercy to us all—Melanesians, Pitcairners and all; and that I needed the discipline I know full well.

To Miss Yonge, on hearing of her Mother's Illness.

1868.

I add one line to assure you of my prayers being offered for you, now more especially when a heavy trial is upon you, and a deep sorrow awaiting you. May God comfort and bless you! Perhaps the full experience of such anxiety, and the pressure of a constant weight may, in His good providence, qualify you more than ever to help others by words put into your mouth out of your own heart-felt troubles. Yet in whatever form the sorrow comes, there is the blessing of knowing that she is only being mysteriously prepared for the life of the world to come. There is no real sorrow where there is no remorse, nor misery for the falling away of those we love. You have, I dare say, known, as I have, some who have the bitterness of seeing their children turn out badly, and this is the sorrow that breaks one down.

Christmas Day, 1868.

My dearest Sisters,

What a happy, happy day! At 12.5 a.m. I was awoke by a party of some twenty Melanesians, headed by Mr. Bice, singing Christmas carols at my bedroom door. It is a glass window, opening on to the verandah. How delightful it was! I had gone to bed with the book of praise by my side, and Mr. Keble's hymn in my mind; and now the Mota versions, already familiar to us, of the angels' song, and of the "Light to lighten the Gentiles," sung, too, by some of our heathen scholars, took up as it were the strain. Their voices sounded so fresh and clear in the still midnight, the perfectly clear sky, the warm, genial climate. I lay awake afterwards thinking on the blessed change wrought on their minds, thinking of my happy lot, of how utterly undeserved it was and is, and (as is natural) losing myself in thoughts of God's wonderful goodness and mercy and love. . . . If you had been here to-day, you would indeed have been full of surprise and thankfulness and hope. There is, I do think, a great deal to show that these scholars of ours so connect religion with all that is cheerful and happy. There is nothing, as I think, sanctimonious about them. They say, "We are so happy here!" How different from our lands! And I think I can truly say that this is not from want of seriousness in those of an age to be serious.

I pour this out to you in my happy day—words of hope and joy and thankfulness! But, remember, that I feel that all this should make me thoughtful, as well as hopeful. How can I say but what sorrow and trial may even now be on their way hither? But I thank God, oh! I do thank Him, for His great love and mercy, and I do not think it wrong to give my feelings of joy some utterance.

1869.

There is, perhaps, no such thing as teaching civilization by word of command, nor religion either. The *sine quâ non* for the missionary—religious and moral character assumed to exist—is the living with his scholars as children of his own. And the aim is to lift them up, not by words, but by the daily life, to the sense of their capacity for becoming by God's grace all that we are, and I pray God a great deal more—not as literary men and scholars, but as Christian men and women, better suited for work than we are among their own people. "They shall be saved even as we." They have a strong sense of and acquiescence in their own inferiority. If we treat them as inferiors, they will always remain in that position of inferiority. But Christ humbled Himself and became the servant and minister, that He might make us children of God and exalt us. It is surely very simple that, if we do thus live among them, they must necessarily adopt some of our habits. Our Lord led the life of a poor man, but He raised His disciples to the highest pitch of excellence by His life, by His words, and His Spirit, the highest that man could receive and follow. The analogy is surely a true one. And exclusiveness and all the pride of race must disappear before such considerations. But it is not the less true that He did not make very small demands upon His disciples, and teach them and us that it needs but little care and toil and preparation to be a Christian, and a teacher of Christianity. The direct contrary of this is the truth. The teacher's duty is to be always leading on his pupils to higher conceptions of their work in life, and to a more diligent performance of it. How can he do this if he himself acquiesces in a very imperfect knowledge and practice of his duty?

To his Sister.

Advent, 1870.

I think that self-consciousness, a terrible malady, is one's misfortune as well as one's fault. But the want of any earnest effort at correcting a fault is worse, perhaps, than the fault itself. And I feel such great, such very great need, for amendment here. This great fault brings its punishment in part even now. I mean there is a want of brightness, cheerfulness, elasticity of mind about the conscious man or woman. He is prone to have gloomy, narrow, sullen thoughts, to brood over fancied troubles and difficulties; because, making everything refer to and depend on self, he naturally can get none of that comfort which they enjoy whose minds naturally turn upwards for help and light. In this way I do suffer a good deal. My chariot wheels often drag very heavily. And yet I know that I am writing now under the influence of a depressing disorder, and that I may misinterpret my real state of mind. No one ought to be happier, so far as advantages of employment in a good service, and kindness of friends, can contribute to make one happy. And on the whole, I know my life is a happy one. I am sure that I have a far larger share of happiness than falls to the lot of most people. Only I do feel very much the lack, almost the utter lack, of that grace which was so characteristic of our dear father, that simplicity and real humility and truthfulness of character! Well, one does not often say these things to another person. But it is a relief to say them. I know the remedy quite well. It is a very simple case for the doctor to deal with, but it costs the patient just everything short of life, when you have to dig right down, and cut out by the roots an evil of a whole life's standing. I assure you it is hard work, because these feelings of ours are such intangible, intractable things. It is hard to lay hold of and mould and direct them. But I pray God that I may not willingly yield to these gloomy, unloving feelings. As often as I look out of myself upon Him, His love and goodness, then I catch a bright gleam. I have much need of your prayers, indeed, for grace and strength to correct faults of which I am conscious, to say nothing of unknown sin.

THE END.

www.ingramcontent.com/pod-product-compliance
Lightning Source LLC
Chambersburg PA
CBHW030359230426
43664CB00007BB/663